The Early Years Communication Handbook

A practical guide to creating a communication friendly setting

Janet Cooper BSC (hons), Reg. MRCSLT

Published by Practical Pre-School Books
St Jude's Church, Dulwich Road, Herne Hill, London, SE24 0PB
Tel. 020 7738 5454
www.practicalpreschoolbooks.com
© MA Education 2010

Illustrations by Cathy Hughes. Front cover image © iStockphoto.com/Katerina Monakhova

The Early Years Communication Handbook ISBN: 978 1 90724 103 1

Introduction

This book is for all early years practitioners and aims to help children develop their listening, understanding, speaking and communication skills. It is particularly useful for staff working in children's centres, nurseries, childminder settings, schools and any other environment implementing the *Every Child a Talker* National Strategy.

Many handbooks and textbooks have made language learning seem much too theoretical and mysterious. There is no mystery to communication development, just good common sense. This guide is designed to support anyone working with children in the early years to develop confidence in early communication development. There is no major cost or piece of equipment needed; the only requirement is your time.

Why is communication important?

All strands of the *Early Years Foundation Stage* (EYFS) (2007) highlight the importance of communication development. A recent review commissioned by the Government identified that 'the ability to communicate is an essential life skill for all children and young people and it underpins a child's social, emotional and educational development' (Bercow, 2008). This review highlighted that any difficulties with communication development can have an impact on all areas of development. *The Rose Review* (2005) states that 'language skills are a foundation for the development of literacy skills' and that 'listening and speaking are the roots of reading and writing.' Until we develop children's communication skills fully, they are unable to reach their full potential in reading and writing. This can only be achieved through a nurturing and stimulating environment which responds to the child's needs. Children are like seeds for beautiful flowers. They are pre-programmed to grow but need all the right conditions to flourish to their full potential.

Communication difficulties are the most common developmental difficulties in children. It is estimated that around 10% of children nationally have significant difficulty with speech and language development (Lyndsay and Dockrell, 2002). These children may require ongoing specialist help. There are also many more children who start school with delayed language skills because of lack of quality stimulation or consistent responsive parenting. The charity ICAN estimates that around half of children entering nursery may have 'transient' speech and language difficulties. 'Transient' speech and language difficulties are when children appear to

be progressing slowly against developmental norms but then 'catch up' eventually. This sometimes happens when children have had an illness or family event, which temporarily affects their developmental progress.

What difference does it make?

Children who have difficulty developing communication skills may have difficulty in all areas of learning but especially social and emotional development. The child who is struggling with communication development may withdraw from communication opportunities or may behave in an aggressive manner to avoid the feeling of inadequacy that communication difficulties can bring. This insecurity puts a child in a state of high anxiety and while in this state the child's emotions are hijacked by a stress response which obstructs listening, attention and learning.

Why do children have communication difficulties?

There are many reasons for delayed communication skills. It is thought that around 5 to 10% of children nationally have medical, neurological or genetic difficulties which require specialist intervention. These children will always need additional help no matter how good the parents or the setting are. However there are a high proportion of children who are born with the potential to develop normally but never reach their full potential. The ICAN *Cost to the Nation* report (2007) describes these children as having 'impoverished language'.

There are also many influences in society that can hinder children's development. Children are bombarded with background noise from stereos, television, computer games and many other gadgets. This has been described as 'toxic childhood' (Palmer, 2007). In isolation, these things may not have a detrimental effect, but when combined, can have significant consequences on children's development. There is also a culture of speaking less to children, for example babies and children who are quiet are often described as 'good children', which reinforces this myth. Many parents still believe that a baby will be 'spoiled' if picked up too much. In fact current research indicates that the more love, touch and affection shown to a baby the more settled and independent he/she will become.

What is the role of the early years practitioner and the setting?

While children are in an early years setting the practitioners take on the role of 'carers'. The way in which staff respond to and engage with children has a major impact on children's development. An EPPE (Effective Provision for Pre-School Education) study, conducted in 2003, highlighted that better trained and skilled early years practitioners led to better outcomes for children. The study found that good quality pre-school experiences support children's social and emotional development, going on to support communication development. Children hold memories of their earliest experiences for life and these shape the brain's growth and development, particularly in the first three years of life.

The role of the early years professional is absolutely crucial to help children reach their full potential. This handbook has been developed to support this role and make communication 'everybody's business'.

How to use this book

Each section of this book contains information, 'Top tips' and photocopiable handouts to use in the setting or home. The theory is supported with practical ideas to make the book easier to dip in and out of. This book is designed to be a useful resource that practitioners can keep returning to for ideas and information as needed.

For the purpose of the book the term 'parent' refers to any adult acting in the role of the parents; this applies to adoptive or foster parents and those looking after children in care.

'Practitioner' refers to any person working directly with children and their families.

'Setting' refers to the place where work takes place, and for some practitioners this may be in the home.

Contents

The book is organised into six main sections:

- The basics of good communication.

- Are you communication friendly?

- Creating a communication friendly environment.

- Ages and stages.

- Involving parents and carers.

- Communication development in a multicultural society.

The basis of good communication

This section covers the elements that make up communication, provides the theory of which skills to develop first and highlights the importance of communication development to children's development as a whole. It provides ideas for activities to try and links to Chapter 3, which describes games to play to help children progress.

There are a number of developmental skills that children need to develop to become effective communicators. Each skill is dependent on the skill before it, but many of these develop at the same time.

Interaction

Communication is made up of a range of skills. It starts with the ability to interact through taking turns and responding to other people. This happens from before birth, with the baby responding to the mother's moods and movements. Babies are pre-programmed to interact and communicate. It is part of their basic survival mechanism.

As children develop and grow they use communication as a means to have their needs met. This often starts with crying to indicate needs, and develops to include non-verbal behaviours, such as smiling and grimacing, and eventually gestures. Parents are not automatically in tune with their baby's cries at birth; it takes time to read the baby's cues and to learn from trial and error. The more time a parent spends with their child the better they get to know their child's needs.

This holds true for practitioners too. For example, children in early years settings can sound unclear or do not have the correct vocabulary to express themselves; this may lead to frustration and may affect the child's behaviour; it is only through developing a relationship with children and observing them that the practitioner can get to know the way they communicate.

Children with speech and language difficulties may demonstrate difficulties forming relationships. Encourage children to express themselves through a variety of non-verbal and verbal means so that they get opportunities to have successful interactions. Games that encourage looking at each other, turn taking, smiling and sharing can help with this. It is also important that the adult interacting with the child is responsive and looks out for all these clues no matter how subtle.

Play

Once a child has begun to interact he/she tests out the relationship through play. Play gives children a chance to explore the world and to try out different types of experiences. Play like all areas of development has a set order in which it develops but individual children will demonstrate a preference for certain types of play. This is dependent on personality, experience and the opportunities children have access to. Children need to learn to explore and to realise cause and effect before they can develop imaginative play. Children do not make a distinction between play and work and neither should practitioners (EYFS, 2007). Practitioners must not underestimate the tremendous amount of learning that takes place through exploring and playing in a range of situations. Play is vital to developing the potential of all children and offers them the chance to be in control. It also co-ordinates learning (Bruce, 2001).

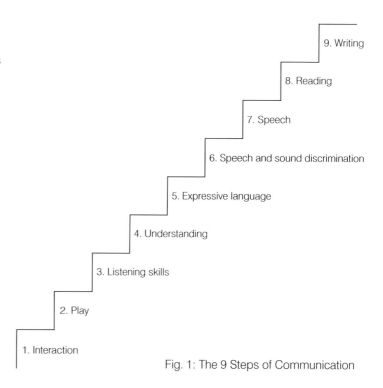

Fig. 1: The 9 Steps of Communication

1. Interaction
2. Play
3. Listening skills
4. Understanding
5. Expressive language
6. Speech and sound discrimination
7. Speech
8. Reading
9. Writing

During play children are able to meet their own needs and to make sense of their own world. Play involves exploring feelings, ideas, materials, relationships and roles. It also helps them make connections between experiences, ideas, objects and environments.

As they get older children begin to develop storylines in their play; this is a vital foundation for writing. A responsive adult can help to extend play to offer new experiences and to build up opportunities for communication to be developed in a natural way. The EYFS supports a child-led approach to child development. Practitioners are encouraged to observe individual children at play, making notes of the types of play they are drawn to and how they interact during play. These observations can help to plan how to move children on and how to extend the play to other levels.

This section could have a few illustrations of children at various play stages eg. baby building tower of bricks, two toddlers playing alongside each other on water play, two children dressing up together and talking to each other.

Case study: Claire, aged two years and four months, was observed at play and showed a preference for sand play. She spent the first day exploring the sand and spent a long time pouring the sand from one container to another. The nursery practitioner added a wider range of containers and sieves for the second day to encourage Claire to explore further. The practitioner played alongside Claire at first and then offered her some commentary on what she was doing. When Claire showed an interest in the practitioner's commentary the practitioner started to ask simple general questions about Claire's play. As Claire's play extended beyond the sand she demonstrated using some of the language she had heard into other situations.

Case study: Joe, aged three years and four months, was observed using DUPLO bricks; he was using them to pretend to 'stamp' the other children. The practitioner made printing stamps and paper available for the following day to extend Joe's interest. Joe was immediately drawn to the stamps and used

these to pretend to play 'post offices'; he requested 'purple paper' for the following day!

Play is learned through various social stages, but how quickly depends on a number of factors, such as the experiences a child is exposed to; the type of emotional attachments formed; the care received; and the level of opportunities for playing with other children.

Having knowledge of 'normal' stages of play is crucial for early years practitioners. It is essential not to have unrealistic expectations of children. For example, it would be quite normal for a child under two to show little interest in other children during play and he/she is very unlikely to share toys. Practitioners should make themselves familiar with children's play patterns and ensure they give children a variety of opportunities to move onto the next stage.

Types of play and their stages:

Manipulative/exploratory play

The child:

- Plays with objects but makes non-specific actions with them, e.g. mouthing, waving and banging toys

- Examines the toy/object

- Plays with objects using appropriate actions, such as shaking rattles (this is an early stage of play usually seen in young babies)

Organising play

The child:

- Relates toys/objects non-specifically to each other, e.g. piling them up

Did you know?

A baby can hear from around 24 weeks in the womb? Newborn babies also demonstrate that they can recognise familiar voices while in the womb. Encourage parents to talk and sing to their bump!

Top tip

Spend time observing children in a range of situations. Make a note of the way they interact with others. Note if there are particular people a child shows a preference for interacting with. This will help you plan for future activities and will enable you to encourage the child's language to develop.

I wonder what she is trying to tell me.

- Systematically combines objects, e.g. stacks cups, builds blocks

Structured or constructional play

The child:

- Fits objects together by trial and error, e.g. DUPLO bricks

- Completes simple boards or puzzles

- Begins to plan how to construct things, e.g. looking to see where shapes fit before posting them into a shape sorter

Cause and effect play

The child:

- Makes a toy work, e.g. presses a button to make a jack in the box pop up

- Uses an object to obtain an item, e.g. uses an umbrella to pull a toy within reach

- Uses an object specifically with another object, e.g. rolls a ball to knock skittles down

Interactive play

The child:

- Tolerates adult presence during play

- Allows an adult to intervene in play

- Will give adult an object during play

- Participates in rough and tumble play

- Allows an adult to imitate his/her action in play

- Responds with anticipation to play routines; e.g. round and round the garden

- Indicates for games to continue

- Initiates games/routines

- Will take turns in play

Pretend play (functional)

The child:

- Uses objects out of context and without situational cues, e.g. takes empty cup to mouth

- Will play functionally with objects, e.g. gives doll a drink, pushes car into a garage

Fig. 2: Social play development

Stage of play	Approximated age	Description
Solitary	0-24 months	Children play alone. There is little interaction with other children.
Spectator	24-30 months	Children will watch other children playing around them.
Parallel	30-36 months	Children will play alongside others but do not play together.
Associative	36-48 months	Children begin to interact with others in play and there may be fleeting co-operation between children in play. Children start to develop friendships and preferences for playing with certain other children.
Co-operative	4+ years	Children play together with shared goals. Play can be quite complicated and children are supportive towards others in their play.

Top tip

Make sure children have access to a range of real objects as well as 'play materials', covering a range of textures, smells, sounds and different visual elements. Many children have limited play experience at home (electronic gadgets or all plastic toys) so it is important to increase the range of play equipment used in the setting.

Top tips for play

- Play must be open ended; there should be no required outcome for everyone to achieve

- Remember that children's play always has a purpose for the child (the child who seems to be aimlessly pouring water may be practising new skills, reliving experiences or calming himself)

- The learning that takes place through play is often hidden; practitioners should not be swayed to do more paper-based activities just because the learning is not taking place in an obvious way

■ Will use miniature representational toys, e.g. PLAYMOBIL® or small world play

Pretend play (symbolic)

The child:

■ Uses the toy as if it were something else, e.g. a brush for a microphone

■ Pretends to play with an absent object, e.g. feeds toys imaginary food

■ Engages in linked sequences of actions, e.g. takes a doll for a walk to the park, goes on swings, goes home to bed

■ Will make the toy be something else, e.g. mum/policeman

■ Will make the toy feel something, e.g. crying/angry

■ Will make a toy act upon an imaginary object

Pretend play (fantasy)

The child:

■ Will pretend to be someone/something else

■ Will do something to or with an imaginary object

■ Adopts and acts out the role for sequences in the play

Pretend play (social)

The child:

■ Has little contact with peers

■ Watches peers playing

■ Is involved in some parallel play

■ Takes part in brief exchanges

■ Can have joint focus in play

■ Carries out role enactment

■ Sustains role play

How can the school/nursery environment be set up to encourage all aspects of play?

All areas of learning should have equal status and should be easily accessible to accommodate all children, no matter what stage they are at. Early years settings need to provide children with opportunities to develop further. For example, practitioners should ensure that children have opportunities for both indoor and outdoor learning, covering:

- Imaginative play (dressing up, PLAYMOBIL®, farms, tea sets)

- Construction: DUPLO, blocks, jigsaws, popoids

- Creative play: clay, paint, play dough, sand

- Physical play: slides, hoops, bikes, skipping ropes.

Practioners can use observations of children to identify which type of play they engage in and look at which level they are at. This will help with the planning of activities to move children to the next stage. Within a setting, children will be at various stages of development and providing a range of activities will accommodate this variety. For example, sometimes simple changes like creating smaller or more nurturing spaces for imaginative play can make a huge difference to how the children access the space. Some of the best equipment for play is natural material rather than bought toys. Adults regularly observe children showing a preference for playing with a cardboard box rather than the toy it contained. By ensuring that children have access to natural non-directive items such as boxes and cartons, practitioners can give the children opportunities to develop their imaginations rather than be led by the limitations of a toy.

Play gives an insight into all areas of a child's development. Through play, practitioners can observe how well a child manipulates toys, talks about them, associates with them and whether they encourage others to join in. It is important to make note of specific things observed, for example a child in the role-play area may struggle to get the dressing-up clothes on, which might indicate the need to encourage motor-skill development.

Children who have speech and language delay may also have delay with play development. Many communication skills can be demonstrated and taught through modelling play to them. Children learn best through fun and games but clear language targets can also be built into play sessions. For example, if a practitioner observes that a child has difficulty with turn-taking skills, he/she can introduce specific games, which require turn taking. This may be something as simple as sharing out the pieces of a jigsaw or shape sorter and taking turns to put the pieces back in.

Listening skills

Listening skills are fundamental to communication development. Babies can hear long before they are born, they are constantly

bombarded by noises from within and outside womb. Studies have demonstrated that they can recognise familiar sounds and voices at birth. By eight to twelve months of age, children begin to develop 'selective attention', which means they are able to tune into the more important sounds and concentrate on those over the less important ones.

When selective attention develops it gives a child more opportunities to concentrate on speech and language, particularly if he/she is spoken to directly. Children mirror the communication they receive. Some children do not develop selective attention by the age of one and studies have indicated that this may have a detrimental affect on their language development. There are many reasons for this delay, such as genetic or neurological problems, which need attention. Other reasons include hearing loss; environmental impacts (such as high levels of background noise); lack of a key carer in close proximity; and lack of stimulating voices and sounds to listen to.

Many homes have high levels of conflicting sounds, such as people talking and moving around; television; computer games; music systems; household appliances and so on. A young child growing up in this kind of environment will find it hard to develop selective attention unless there is a responsive adult explaining the sounds along with opportunities for quiet times. It would be unrealistic to expect families to never have the television on or never listen to music but families do need to know that quiet times are important for early child development and that sustained and increased background noises can have long term negative effects on children's development. The message is to ensure that young children have lots of opportunities for listening time.

Many children have poor listening skills due to glue ear. Glue ear is the most common childhood illness and children under the age of five are the largest affected group (though for some it can persist into adolescence). Glue ear can cause temporary deafness, delayed speech and language and affect children's behaviour. It is caused by fluid blocking the middle ear, which means sound is not transmitted properly to the inner ear. The most common contributing factors for this are colds and flu, passive smoking, poor hygiene of things like dummies and bottles, and genetic conditions such as a cleft palate.

If a child has delayed listening skills he/she may find it especially difficult to settle in to a task and actively listen while in a setting. In these instances it is even more important that settings are arranged to encourage active listening and quiet times. Having a radio on in the background may be interesting to the staff of a nursery, or a childminder in the home, but it may interfere with children's listening development. Practitioners should only introduce background music if it has a purpose, for example to calm children when they come in after lunch, or as a trigger for tidying up. The use of television within settings should also be minimized (for childminders this may mean limiting the use of television in their own homes). In all settings, using the television should have a clear purpose and programmes should be chosen carefully for suitable content. Practitioners should sit alongside children so that they can talk about the programmes and follow up the children's interests by extending the characters into play. Practitioners need to make sure that the parents and carers of children they work with know how important listening development is and that they can support this through offering quiet times and listening times.

Case study: Robert, aged two years and eight months was visited at home by a play and learning team from a children's centre. He was referred because of limited play experience and poor language development. On the first visit it became apparent that the television was on in the background for a significant part of the day. When questioned, his mother reported that they put the television on in the background when they got up in the morning and left it on for the whole day. If they tried to turn it off Robert had a 'tantrum'. The children's centre worker explained the importance of developing listening skills for language to develop and worked with the family to reduce the amount of television time. Robert was encouraged to access a 'play bag' on loan from the centre. The television was turned off when the play bag (full of toys) was introduced. Robert was so engrossed with the toys and the Play Worker that he did not notice the television being turned off. His mother was shown how to use the toys in a variety of ways and was eventually able to introduce a play bag on a daily basis with the television turned off. Robert's language skills developed quickly following this. His mother was so impressed by his development from using the play bags that she started to attend a regular toddler group at the children's centre as well.

Listening skills and concentration can also be affected by over-stimulating a child visually. Many settings have very creative staff; they love the children to produce pictures and models and use every spare space to display work. Children with poor listening skills often need a less distracting environment for them to fully concentrate and listen. Visual displays are fine for the majority of a setting but practitioners should make sure there is a plainer area provided so that children can carry out listening tasks. If space is short, an area can be sectioned off with a large piece of material or by using a 'pop up' tent to create an uncluttered listening area.

Activity

Stop for one minute and actively listen to the sounds around you. Initially, you will notice louder or more prominent sounds, but as you concentrate you will realise that you are also tuning into quieter and less obvious sounds like your own breathing. You learned the skill of identifying which were the important sounds very early in life. Children who are delayed in this area find it hard to concentrate and are easily distracted. This can have a major impact on the way they learn language and how they communicate.

Did you know?

Research suggests that breastfeeding may reduce the risk of babies and young children developing glue ear. It is thought that breast milk contains protein, which can help stop inflammation and help protect against glue ear even when breastfeeding has stopped.

The physical layout of a room or building can also affect listening skills. With large open-plan areas try creating some smaller, more nurturing spaces with the use of materials like voile, large boxes or even turning furniture around to create smaller spaces.

Listening skills will also have a major impact on children's comprehension development.

Understanding language

Comprehension of language means understanding language and this process is often called 'receptive' language. This is when the brain makes sense of verbal and non-verbal information. Language comprehension is reliant on accurate messages reaching the brain and is dependent on good listening skills.

Understanding language is probably the most complicated thing that we do as human beings. Comprehension follows a set pattern for most children and begins by understanding the situation, for example a child may learn to brush their hair with a brush before they can label the brush or answer questions about it. Children then learn vocabulary; a set of names to label things. The size of a child's vocabulary is dependant on the experiences he/she has and the responsiveness of the carer. For example, a child being pushed along in a buggy may see a dog run past; if the carer follows the child's observation and remarks 'oh look there's a dog' the child eventually learns to associate what he/she is seeing with the label the carer gives to it. If a carer is in tune with a child's interests and offers a model of language, the child will quickly learn to associate and attach words to things and experiences.

A study by Biemiller (2003) indicates that vocabulary is a strong determiner of reading success. Both parents and practitioners have a crucial role in developing children's vocabulary. Biemiller noted that vocabulary growth is largely determined by parental

practises, particularly before the age of seven. The good news is that teaching vocabulary can have a huge impact on children's reading comprehension. Practitioners and parents can make sure that children have a range of experiences, and that these experiences are repeated in different ways so that children hear the language in different formats and contexts. For example, a child who has learnt to label a real dog also needs to learn that a picture of a dog is given the same label. The child also needs to hear other words that are associated with it, such as the dog's colour, sound and size.

Once children have a core vocabulary they start to recognise the words they know in different sentences and situations. They learn that certain words go together and learn to associate verbs (action words) and adjectives (describing words) to them. In normal development children tend to learn nouns (naming words) first, then verbs then adjectives. This point is worth noting in relation to children who are still developing language or have delayed language skills. Many practitioners launch into teaching colours (adjectives) to children who have no range of nouns to link the colours to. This will have little meaning to the child and will result in a very slow route to language learning. If a child is markedly delayed with language skills, the practitioner should make a list of the types of words that would be useful on a daily basis and make sure that these are used in context as often as possible.

Once children understand single words they start to pick out key words within sentences; at first, they understand two key words, then eventually three and four. Once children can follow these simple sentence structures they start to learn the 'rules' of language, known as 'grammar' or 'syntax'. Different languages vary in their rules, and children with access to more than one language may try to apply the rules of their main language to their second language.

Other than understanding words and sentences, children need to assess situations and pick up on non-verbal cues. These may include body language, such as facial expressions, posture, gestures, and tone of voice. Children learn non-verbal cues through regular and close contact with an interactive carer . Routines help support this process as children learn to associate language with certain situations and have opportunities to practise repetition.

Visual timetables (pictures showing the key routines of the day) and picture labels are a good way of giving children additional information about their environment and help to support them in learning routines and vocabulary. Refer to picture labels and visual timetables regularly, talk to children about them and use

the same words to describe them. Children with significant language delay may need just a couple of pictures to start with and then further additions as they become familiar with the routine and the language. Photographs of actual objects or persons can also be very effective as some children are not ready to recognise pictures. For these children, a practitioner may need to provide an object to symbolize an event, such as a hand towel and soap to indicate hand washing, or a toy spider to indicate singing 'incey wincey spider'. These cues need to be used consistently and repeatedly alongside talk so that children learn to recognise the appropriate associations between pictures and what they mean.

Checklist for comprehension: If a child does not seem to understand what is being said to them, check the following:

- Can the child hear?

- Does he/she have difficulties with listening skills?

- Is the setting's environment set out to encourage good listening?

- Does the child understand a wide range of vocabulary?

- What should the child understand for their age and how far from this do they appear to be? (See Chapter 3)

- Does the child's development seem to be following a normal pattern at a slower rate, or an unusual pattern?

- Does he/she understand situations and routines?

- Is the child able to follow non-verbal routines and instructions?

- Is he/she familiar with English or do they have another language they are more confident in?

- Do the child's parents have any concerns?

- Do picture cues help the child understand?

Referral indicators:

- Unusual patterns of development

- Child making little or no progress despite offering a range of stimulating activities

- Parental concern

- Child struggling to access the curriculum as a result of their comprehension difficulties

- Child showing frustration at his/her lack of understanding

Some children with receptive (understanding) difficulties will be 'echolalic', meaning that they will echo back the words said to them without understanding them. These children often have clear speech and can imitate sentences but do not understand the words that are spoken to them. If a practitioner has any concerns regarding this they should always seek an additional opinion.

A child's play can often give insights into his/her language development. If children are at a symbolic level of play this demonstrates that they are able represent the world through objects and toys. Once children are able to do this they show that they are ready to represent objects through words.

Alongside understanding words and sentences children need to pick up non-verbal cues, such as facial expression, tone of voice, and gestures. Children learn to 'cue read' from birth and babies are born with a reflex that is interested in faces. Studies have demonstrated that new-born babies show a preference for face shapes when given a choice between face patterns and similar patterns in a different order. How well babies turn this reflex into a developing skill depends entirely on the responsiveness of their carers. If a carer spends his/her time making regular eye contact and talking frequently to a child, the child learns to link the carer's cues with various situations, experiences and feelings. Although parents are usually the primary carers, practitioners take on this role within settings. It is vital for practitioners to share their observations with parents to get a full picture of a child's ability.

Expressive language

'Expressive language' is the output of language. Children use language to express their wants, needs and their emotions. As children become more proficient with language they are able to use it to control, discuss, argue and debate.

Expressive language mirrors comprehension development. Children usually begin by making sounds. They learn that sounds carry meaning and as they start to understand the words spoken to them they begin to use the sounds in strings to create words. First words are usually determined by a child's environment. If a parent or carer reacts positively when a baby makes sounds or attempts to communicate this reinforces the communication and encourages the baby to do it again. Sadly, many early communication attempts are misinterpreted or ignored and children are often given a dummy when they attempt to express themselves. This results in children learning not to express themselves.

Top tips for expressive language

- Make time for talking

- Show the child you are interested in what he/she is trying to tell you

- Follow the child's lead but give names to things that he/she is interested in

- Add words to extend children's sentences; if a child says 'look car' say 'yes it's a red car'

- Talk about things as they are happening, this will give children labels to attach to things in context and will encourage them to talk

- Minimize use of dummies and try to get rid of them completely by the age of 12 months

- With young babies try to work out what their cries are trying to tell you by being familiar with their routine.

Top tip

Any concerns about a child's understanding of language should be shared with the child's parents. Many receptive language (comprehension) difficulties go undetected for quite a while as children often compensate by imitating others. This can have a significant impact on a child's learning. Some children may need to be referred to a speech and language therapist for further assessment.

Many parents and carers worry that they do not know what their young babies are trying to tell them when they are crying. It takes time to tune into a baby or young child but with perseverance and time, parents and carers will learn to read cues. Parents, carers and practitioners should not interfere with any attempts a baby or child makes at communicating. Providing a dummy might interfere with the carer being able to understand the child, therefore not being able to meet the child's needs.

Speech sound discrimination

Part of the process of understanding language and learning to turn this into meaningful speech is the ability to distinguish between different sounds; some of these differences are very fine. Children have to learn that sounds may be made in a similar way but that slight differences between them can change the meaning of what is said. For example, the sounds 'p' and 'b' are made by putting the lips together and making a short burst of sound. The only difference between them is that 'p' does not have a voice and 'b' does have a voice. This will make a huge difference to the meaning when put into a word, for example 'pea' versus 'bee'.

When children are starting out with language development they often make mistakes in their output of sounds. This is an ongoing process; children need opportunities to hear language spoken around them and they will eventually get better at sound discrimination. Children are generally better at discriminating sounds at the beginning of words, then the ends, and finally the middle. Singing nursery rhymes and songs can help fine tune sound awareness and is a fun way of teaching the rhythm of language. Music can enhance social development and may also have a positive physiological impact.

Did you know?

A study by Hart and Risley in America in 1995 found that children whose parents spoke more to them in the early years a wider vocabulary, went on to have a higher IQ and achieved more at school.

Did you know?

In normal development children understand words before they can say them.

Did you know?

The average child says their first word at around 12 months old?

Speech

Many people get confused between the terms 'speech' and 'language'. They are actually very different but intimately linked. 'Speech' is the term used to describe the sounds made with the mouth, lips, teeth, tongue, palate and nose. When these sounds are linked together they form words, which are the units of 'language'.

'Language' is the understanding and use of these words for communication. For example, take the word 'frembovonombardo'; it is difficult to pronounce but the chances are that with a little practise most people would be able to say this word even though it is completely made up. This demonstrates speech ability. Speech requires a person to move various parts of the mouth co-ordinated with breathing and voice to make sounds. Now if someone is asked the question 'How many frembovonombardo does it take to build a wall?'; the question cannot be answered because the word has no meaning. This demonstrates understanding 'language' and using words to communicate.

Children tend to develop speech at different rates but there are recognised patterns to the order in which speech sounds develop. How quickly children pick up the sounds depends on a variety of factors. Medical and genetic conditions may affect production of speech. For example, many children with Down's Syndrome have large tongues, a pronounced bottom jaw, and low oral muscle tone which can affect speech development. This may automatically put the child at risk of speech difficulties. Any structural change in the mouth can have a dramatic affect on speech, such as gaps in teeth, protruding jaws, poor muscle tone or any restriction of tongue movement. Any difficulties with hearing or listening can also have an affect on speech production. These risks need to be minimized as much as possible and practitioners should share any concerns with parents, GPs or Health Visitors.

Case study: Jack, aged three years and two months, lived at home with his mother and younger brother. He made good eye contact, played well with his brother and children at the nursery; he was lively and sociable. He appeared to understand most of what was said to him, could talk in sentences stringing four to five words together and was developing imaginative sequences of play. His listening was variable and his speech attempts were very unclear.

The nursery practitioner observed that Jack was unable to make adults understand what he was saying and that the children were also struggling to understand him. Jack was reacting to this with frustration. The nursery practitioner made a series of observations in a range of situations. She met with Jack's parents to discuss her concerns and to establish whether the parents were concerned and if there was any underlying condition, which may be influencing the situation.

The discussion revealed that Jack had previously suffered with heavy colds and glue ear which was now getting better. They agreed that the nursery would offer a range of daily listening activities for Jack and would ensure that he had lots of opportunities to be face to face with an adult for talking

Top tips for speech

- Encourage all attempts at talking, even if speech is unclear

- Reduce the amount of time children use dummies and aim to completely get rid of them by the age of 12 months

- Respond to children's attempts to talk

- If a child makes a mistake with speech do not correct him/her, just repeat the word back accurately (e.g., if a child says 'pish' for 'fish', say 'yes it's a fish')

- If a child's speech is very unclear, provide a home-setting diary for parents to give additional information about what has gone on beyond the setting (this will help give the child additional context to his/her speech)

- If speech sounds are persistently unclear (especially to familiar adults) seek advice from a Health Visitor or school nurse; referral to speech and language therapy may be necessary activities. The parents also agreed to make some quiet times at home for reading stories with Jack to give him more opportunities to hear speech patterns. When he was reviewed six weeks later Jack had made significant progress with his listening skills, and some progress with his speech.

Reading and writing

Reading and writing are additional ways of communicating. They rely on a child having well-developed verbal skills and internal language (knowing a range of words to represent objects, actions and concepts). Children need to develop all the other steps of communication well before they are ready for reading and writing. If a practitioner is working with a child who is struggling with reading or writing skills, he/she needs to make sure all the other communication steps are developing well.

As with spoken language, written language requires development of vocabulary and rules. It is a high-level skill, which requires a child to have an internal representation of language. If children are not able to comprehend verbal language they will struggle with reading and writing. It is therefore essential to develop spoken language and communication skills first, so that these can be internalized and used later for written language.

A good way of encouraging this internalization is through regular reading to children. When children are read to, they become familiar with hearing the words, associating them to the pictures, hearing the rhythm of speech and they learn that verbal language can be represented by text. The golden rule for both reading and singing is repetition. Children need to hear the same songs and stories over and over again to learn the predictability of the words and to benefit from the vocabulary. Practitioners can extend this further by adding role play to the story and creating storytelling themed activities.

Are you communication friendly?

This section will help practitioners recognise what to look for when conducting an audit of whether or not a setting is communication friendly. Chapter 3 links with this section to provide ideas to help meet some of the criteria.

All practitioners working with young children have a role to play in developing children's communication skills. Whether they work with children and families in a playgroup, toddler group or pre-school setting, practitioners have a unique opportunity to help children develop their full potential. Communication affects feelings and behaviour and so it is vital for an early years setting to be communication friendly.

The general environment

It is essential for parents and children to feel confident when they first enter a setting. The kind of welcome families receive makes all the difference to the relationship a practitioner will have with them. There are a number of simple basics for communication, which create a positive atmosphere for children and families. Is there a friendly face greeting families as they arrive? Is there consistency of staff on reception so that families can recognise and get to know them? How accessible is the building? Will parents and visitors be attended to quickly or will they be left hanging around for a while? If a parent has a poor experience on the first visit this may affect subsequent attendance. Many parents lack the confidence to attend new groups or go to new settings. Often, they are perceived as cliquey or uninviting. A simple way to overcome initial barriers is to offer an introduction session or a home visit to introduce staff and to give families a named person to liaise with. Named key-workers also demonstrate that a setting is approachable and friendly. This all aids transition both for parent and child. Often we underestimate the need for parents to have preparation for transitions and focus all our attention on the child's needs. The better prepared parents are for change the more they can discuss this with their children and prepare them, thus easing the transition.

The communication environment

The 'communication environment' describes the methods, reasons and opportunities children have to communicate within a setting environment and whether these are maximized. Opportunities to communicate do not rely on expensive equipment or planned sessions. Children communicate in response to stimulus, such as something they see, hear, taste, smell or feel; children also communicate when they have needs that they want to express. Practitioners need to be aware of children's experiences and follow their interests. There is no point ploughing on with a colouring task if a child has just heard

a jet plane go overhead and is excited by it. Follow the child's lead. If the child wants to comment on the plane respond to the comments and ask further questions.

Settings need to ensure that stimulating experiences and materials are provided and that someone is available to respond. Sometimes the simplest objects can provide the stimulus for communication; provide materials such as tropical fruit, shells, a bag of dressing-up clothes or a treasure basket. There should be a range of interesting toys and activities within the setting. Use toys that stimulate the senses, but beware that many shop-bought toys restrict the amount of sensory stimulation they provide.

Knowledge and skills

The knowledge and skills of practitioners working with pre-school children can have a major impact on children's development. It is essential that practitioners have extensive knowledge of child development so that they can identify what stages children are at and whether they are developing along normal lines. This knowledge will help indicate whether children need to be referred to other agencies or child care specialists to assist with their development.

The checklists on page 24 will help settings to identify areas for action or training needs. There are a range of resources available to support this (see further reading section page 62) and The Communication Trust (2009) have developed a competencies framework to support practitioners in their development of knowledge and skills. It is important that a setting does not rely on one person to develop knowledge and skills relating to the area of

Make sure you have a range of textures, colours, smells, tastes and sounds within the setting for the child to experience. Link these to any story or role-play themes you may have. Extend the children's interests by following up with other activities, e.g. if you are reading 'The Gingerbread Man' story follow up the story by making ginger bread men together and letting the children taste the biscuits.

Make the most of time with each child. Some of the best communication times are informal and unplanned. This may be when a child is arriving, having a snack, having their nappy changed or playing outside. Think about all the times in a day when you communicate with the children. Are you readily available to listen and respond to them? Do you make the most of every opportunity?

communication. Being communication friendly only works if there is shared responsibility and everyone understands that this is part of their role.

Policy and procedure

Good communication practices need to be built into the policies and procedures of a setting. Putting such information into policy and procedure documents will emphasize the importance of developing communication. Policies should be determined by good practice. For example, practitioners should identify the procedures and activities that works, then turn these into setting policies. It may be worth identifying a policy for 'meet and greet' in the mornings; a policy for key workers or significant carers; a policy on supporting parents and so on. Policies do not need to be lengthy documents; they represent a shared acknowledgement of what works best for the children in a setting.

Use the checklist for policy and procedure on page 25. You may wish to add procedures that you value within your setting as these should be led by evidence-based practice.

Parents as partners

Parents are a child's first educators and it is essential to work alongside them to help children achieve their full potential. It is useful for practitioners to investigate the experiences families and children receive when they attend a setting. Involving parents and children in these discussions is essential to see things from a user's perspective. Questionnaires, whilst giving chance for parents to contribute, can feel very threatening or

Oh look, there's an aeroplane!

may only elicit responses from a vocal few. Coffee mornings may provide greater opportunities for parents to discuss their feelings in an informal atmosphere. The programme 'Stoke Speaks Out' has found that encouraging parents to stay on after a toddler session, over a cup of tea, has enabled parents to have their say. Some settings invite parents to attend a short nursery rhyme performance by their children and then stay for refreshments and a chat about their experiences of the setting.

The ethos of 'parents as partners' must be genuine. Research tells us that the parents have the most influence over child development and so practitioners will serve children better by working in partnership with the parents. Practitioners also need to be mindful of the parents' readiness to engage. If parents do not take part in events or respond to written notes, consider things from their point of view. Do they have time to meet up with you? Can they read? Can they speak English? Do they have any special needs? Are there family circumstances which make engagement difficult? (Such as a new baby, caring for a relative, domestic violence, health issues, unusual working patterns.) It is only by attempting to get to know parents and genuinely valuing their input that practitioners will be able to acknowledge their readiness to engage with the setting.

Positive relationships between staff, parents and children develop an atmosphere of trust. This is the best foundation for developing communication.

Working through the following checklists should help practitioners focus on the strengths and weaknesses of their setting. Settings need to provide a a balance in each area to ensure children and their families get maximum benefit. Fostering good relationships with parents and carers will ensure that children are given the best possible start in life, with rich language opportunities. Some children may be getting additional support from agencies for their communication development. It is essential that practitioners work in partnership with these agencies to maximize the benefit for the child.

Best practice

- Children's work is acknowledged and respected

- Children feel they belong to your setting

- Children develop a sense of identity in your setting

- Staff are approachable

- There is a consistency of staff

- Staff are responsive to the changing needs of both children and parents

- Staff know who the child's key relationships are with

- Staff make efforts to include key carers in conversations with the child

- Each child is seen as unique with their own unique characteristics

- Staff are able to observe which stages of development the child is at, and plan and respond accordingly

What to do if a child is attending speech and language therapy

Children access speech and language therapy if they have a severe delay or disorder of voice, speech, language or fluency. Some children have speech and language therapy if they have feeding or swallowing problems. Practitioners should be aware of the local criteria for accessing these services. Some authorities only treat children with the most marked or profound difficulties, while some only offer the service to children of a particular age group; most speech and language therapy departments will have specific referral criteria. The majority of speech and language therapy services are commissioned through Health Trusts. Some departments will provide a service

suggests a particular programme, discuss how this will fit into the setting's routine and how it might be adapted to fit in. Be aware of any particular targets or particular programmes that the therapist sets. Practitioners may need to attend specific training to help implement these targets and programmes. The practitioner should always encourage parents to attend appointments and explain the benefits for the child and the overall value of therapy.

What do Speech and Language Therapists do?

Children generally follow a set pattern of development for communication. Speech and Language Therapists are trained to identify normal patterns of voice, speech, language, fluency and swallowing. They are also trained to assess these and detect where the pattern of development is delayed or disordered. 'Delay' is when the communication pattern occurs in the usual order but at a slower rate. 'Disorder' is when the child's communication does not follow the normal pattern.

Following assessment, the therapist can give advice and strategies to meet the child's needs. Many therapists act in a consultative and advisory way to support the practitioners who have regular contact with a child. Assessment is usually carried out through play and observations but there are also a range of 'standardized' tests (tests that have been carried out on a wide population and can therefore give a suggested score for a child's age), which they may use. These tests may range from using objects and toys through to pictures and instructions. The therapist will ask the parents a range of questions to establish how the child has developed from birth and how much the communication difficulties impact on the child's life.

in schools and settings, others will offer home visits, and some may be run from a clinic or children's centre.

If a child is referred to speech and language therapy, the practitioner needs to share all relevant information to help the therapist assess the child. This will include background of any relevant family history, social issues (which may affect the family accessing appointments) and how the child behaves in the setting. Relevant medical information, such as, hearing difficulties, persistent colds, breathing difficulties, general ill health, and hospitalisation should also be highlighted. All these factors can affect a child's communication development and will be taken into account during an assessment of the child's needs. Along with a referral it is helpful to state what advice has been given to the family and what strategies have already been tried. Many children respond well to the general good practices outlined in this guide and will make progress as a result. The therapist will need to know if the child is exposed to more than one language and whether the parents will require an interpreter to respond to and attend any appointments.

Practitioners should obtain written consent from parents so that the speech and language therapy service can share information with the setting; it is useful to get this consent at the referral stage. If a child has been referred by another agency, ask the parents for permission to liaise with the therapist. Many Speech and Language Therapists write information into the parent-held record books; ask parents to bring these in to help you become familiar with a child's early development and which agencies are currently involved.

Once a child is attending therapy sessions the practitioner should make contact with the therapist to discuss any plans for the child. It is useful to discuss assessment and treatment plans and also how the child's communication difficulties affect his/her learning, behaviour and relationships within the setting. Ask the therapist for general strategies to support the child on a daily basis and for more specific activities to share with the parents. If the therapist

Which children will access speech and language therapy?

Some difficulties are 'congenital', meaning that they are present from birth and may be part of a syndrome or another recognised disorder. Many of these children will be at risk of communication or feeding difficulties and the therapist may work in a preventative way to minimize the impact of these difficulties. Some communication difficulties are 'developmental', meaning they are not obviously present at birth but as the child develops, the pattern of development is not typical, or is at a dramatically slower rate than average.

Voice difficulties

Voice difficulties occur when a child has a husky or hoarse quality to their voice for a long period. This is not common in children's development and may be linked to inadequate breath support, over-use of the voice (such as shouting) or poor control of the voice, particularly following a period of laryngitis. Some children may have structural abnormalities, which affect the use of the voice. The therapist will detect the symptoms, recommend any exercises and, if required, set up referral to a paediatric Ear, Nose and Throat Surgeon.

Speech difficulties

Speech therapy is generally required when the child is severely delayed or disordered in their speech. A child with a 'specific' speech disorder (such as a severe and complex speech pattern) may need long-term support. The therapy will often include exercises and games to carry out at home or in the setting along with advice for adapting the environment to maximize communication. Children with severe difficulties may need a communication aid or may need to use signs or symbols to supplement their speech or language.

Children with minor speech difficulties generally do not require speech and language therapy. For example, a child who says 'pider' for 'spider' at the age of three-and-a-half years. These children should show progress with their speech over a short period with the help of a practitioner.

Language difficulties

Language difficulties are often marked by poor comprehension and limited expressive language. These can accompany speech difficulties but can be a problem in their own right. Language difficulties may range from not talking at all, to having disordered grammar and poor narrative skills. If the child has ongoing difficulty understanding language and has problems developing sentences, he/she may need a therapist's support.

The majority of children with language difficulties will have problems learning new vocabulary and may find it hard to remember words. Children who are just a little late starting to talk but then suddenly begin communicating do not require speech and language therapy. These children often start out in a setting with delayed language but pick up lots of new words within a few weeks and will catch up over time.

Fluency difficulties

Fluency difficulties are often labelled as stammering or stuttering. This is when the flow of speech is hesitant, blocked, or is repeated regularly. For example, a child may say 'mu, mu, mummy' when attempting to say 'mummy'. There is, however, a normal, non-fluent phase that many children go through as they develop their language; this usually occurs between the ages of two-and-a-half and four-years. This is the period when their brains are trying to process and formulate language very quickly. This normal non-fluent stage still needs to be handled sensitively in the setting environment to ensure children do not develop a stammer.

Practitioners can help to reduce fluency difficulties by taking the following measures:

▩ Make time for talking

▩ Be a good listener when the child is trying to speak

▩ Maintain eye contact with the child

▩ Model slow and unhurried speech to the child

▩ Don't ask the child to repeat what he/she has said, this can lead to additional frustration

▩ Make sure all children get their turns in a conversation

▩ Reduce background noise as much as is possible

▩ Describe inaccurate fluency as 'bumpy talking' to the child; if the child gets upset by the non-fluency be supportive by saying 'don't worry we all get bumpy talking sometimes'

Around 20% of children go through a normal non-fluent phase and the majority of these children grow out of it with careful and supportive parents and carers.

Checklists

The next five pages contain photocopiable checklists designed to enable you to outline where you setting needs to take any action to improve its delivery in the following areas:

▩ partnerships with parents

▩ the communication environment

▩ knowledge of language development and skills

▩ policy and procedures

▩ the general environment

General environmental checklist

Key point	Always	Sometimes	Rarely	Action
Is it obvious how to access the setting?				
Can parents get into the building with a pram or buggy?				
Does your setting have access for parents or children in a wheelchair?				
If parents want to come to you for help can they bring their other children or babies (who may not attend the setting)?				
Are signs presented in basic language with symbols to help those with poor literacy skills or limited English?				
Is there a consistent person(s) to welcome families on arrival?				
Do you make time to talk to parents and children on arrival to discuss any news or issues?				
Do you welcome families with a smile and respond to them in a timely fashion?				
Do your staff have good interaction skills to enable them to communicate with families from a range of backgrounds?				
Are routines and procedures shared with parents and children?				
Are routines supported with visual prompts, e.g. visual timetables?				
Are telephone enquiries dealt with in a timely manner?				

Communication environmental checklist

Key point	Needs developing	Partly developed	Developed
Does your setting provide a range of materials that stimulate all of the senses? (Touch, smell, hearing, sight, taste.)			
Are children encouraged to request things they need? Do you have a range of materials suitable for children's learning stages rather than their ages?			
Does your setting provide opportunities for quiet listening times?			
Do you provide opportunities for talking times?			
Does someone respond when children want to communicate?			
Are you and your staff flexible enough to follow a child's lead even if it deviates from your plans?			
Does your setting provide activities to stimulate listening skills?			
Are all routine activities maximized for communication?			
Do your staff provide strong communication models for the children?			
Do your staff have well-developed communication skills?			
Do staff demonstrate that talking is fun?			
Is there continuity between key staff so that children feel emotionally confident to communicate?			

Knowledge and skills checklist

Key point	Needs developing	Partly developed	Fully developed
Do staff have a basic knowledge of child development?			
Do staff have an awareness of the importance of parents in children's development?			
Do staff know all of the elements that make up communication skills? (Listening, comprehension, expression, speech, verbal and non-verbal communication.)			
Do staff have knowledge of the range of communication difficulties children can encounter?			
Do staff know what to do if they are concerned about a child's communication development?			
Do staff know how to access support for children with communication difficulties?			
Do staff know a range of basic strategies to try when children have communication difficulties?			
Do staff know how to maximize the environment to support children's communication development?			

Policy and procedure checklist

Key point	Needs developing	Partly developed	Fully developed
Are staff aware that communication development is part of their role?			
Do staff make use of every opportunity to encourage communication development?			
Do staff encourage parents to take an active role in their child's development by involving them in activities within the setting, providing information and regularly talking to them?			
Are parents, children and visitors greeted in a consistently friendly, responsive way?			
Do your training plans ensure that staff have adequate training in communication and child development?			
Do your induction policies acknowledge finding out about the level and detail of each child's communication skills? (E.g. their interests, how and why they communicate).			
Are there procedures to highlight and document any concerns regarding children's communication skills?			
Are there procedures in place to pass on any concerns to the relevant agencies?			
Do activities provide opportunities for language learning to be maximized?			
Does your planning reflect observations of children and what is learned from these observations?			
Do new staff have a clear induction programme that reflects and acknowledges children's communication development?			
Are the setting's procedures and policies shared with new staff?			
Are parents valued as partners of the setting?			

Parents as partners checklist

Key point	Not developed	Partly developed	Fully developed
Are parents and carers made to feel welcome in the setting?			
Is information for parents available in a range of formats and on a range of topics relating to child development?			
Are parents made aware of setting routines and changes in advance?			
Are children encouraged to talk about their home life?			
Are parents encouraged to share concerns regarding their children?			
Are parents and children encouraged to share news from home?			
Are parents involved in new developments concerning the setting?			
Do staff share news from the setting with parents?			
Do staff share concerns regarding children with their parents?			
Do staff know the range of cultures and backgrounds the children are from and make efforts to acknowledge these cultures within the setting?			
If parents do not speak English, are efforts made to provide an interpreter or provide information in a relevant format?			

Creating a communication friendly environment

This practical section covers ideas for supporting communication in a setting. It gives ideas for games that develop skills in looking, listening, proximity, sharing interests, giving reasons, and extending opportunities. It also highlights the importance of a setting's whole environment, linking to the theory behind the Early Years Foundation Stage framework.

For a setting to be truly communication friendly all staff need to be aware of the importance of good and positive communication. Being communication friendly relies on an ethos of the whole setting becoming engaged. This involves everything from the setting's signage to the way children and parents are spoken to and the opportunities they are given.

Creating a welcoming environment

First impressions make all the difference. Parents and visitors need to feel welcome when they visit a setting. Try the following ideas to support this:

■ Introduce a 'welcome board'. This can be a whiteboard or a board with removable push-in lettering to keep it up-to-date. Make sure the board welcomes any planned visitors. If there are no planned activities that day just put up a welcome to all parents or a simple message that will make people feel valued.

■ Make sure signage is easy to follow. Make it clear how to get into the building and where to find the reception or members of staff.

■ Make sure signage has simple pictures or instructions, this will help visitors with poor literacy, or who are not familiar with English.

■ Make the entrance into the setting more obvious by painting footsteps or paw prints leading from the path to the door.

■ Make the way into the setting more exciting; involve children in tying coloured ribbons onto trees or lamposts along the path to the door. This could be linked later to themes such as 'going on a bear hunt' or 'finding pirate treasure'.

■ Make sure everyone who receives visitors welcomes them with a smile.

■ Put up pictures of staff with their names in the entrance hall. This will help parents feel more at ease and help them get to know practitioners' names.

■ Have information available on a range of topics for families to take away. Not everyone is confident enough to ask for help but may take information away to look at in the privacy of their own home.

■ Attend to visitors promptly; smile; be friendly; and try to address their needs as quickly as possible.

■ Display children's work and images of them taking part in a range of activities in places where parents can see them and at a height where children can also see them. This makes the children feel valued and reassures parents.

■ Expect most parents to come through the door with their children. Encourage parents to come into the building at the start and end of the day to make them feel welcome.

■ Self-registration is a great way of encouraging parents into a setting. Try having photographs of the child and the parent for the child to find in the morning. When they arrive the child can put their picture onto a separate chart. Ask parents to provide a range of pictures of people who may be collecting the child. In the morning, they could put out the picture of the person who should be collecting the child. This will also help to ease any separation anxiety. Make sure any anxious children are warned if the person picking them up will be different from the one planned.

■ Have a comments book for parents to write how they feel or any questions they have. Turn this into a 'thank you' book or a comments tree (where parents take a cut-out leaf, write their comments on it then tie it to the tree).

- Encourage parents to bring in items from home to support the children's learning. These may be items linked to a topic or photographs for sharing. This shows parents that the home environment is valued. Make a wishing tree on which to hang little notes of items required. The parents take a note away of something they are prepared to bring in.

- Make hanging mobiles for each child. These can have a series of photographs of key people in the child's life; hang them from the ceiling.

- Create a clearly-labelled parent's notice board at a distinctive point near the entrance. Ask parents what information they would find useful to display on the board. Make sure this area has some key tips and advice available for parents. Personalize the board by acknowledging specific news, such as 'Congratulations to Shaun's mummy on the birth of a baby girl'.

If you manage a setting it is useful to ask parents or a visitor to be a 'mystery shopper' to feedback on how they felt when they visited or tried to call. If you have colleagues in a different setting you could carry this out for each other to get neutral feedback.

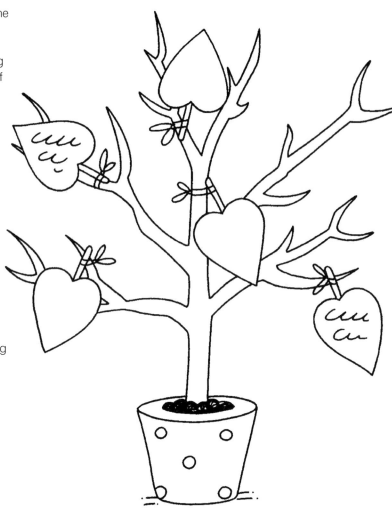

The communication environment

The Early Years Foundation Stage expects 'areas of learning' to be clearly identifiable but it is important to note that communication should take place in all areas not just in the 'Communication, Language and Literacy' area.

Within a setting it is important to ensure opportunities are available to facilitate certain communication skills such as talking, listening and playing. Children need to opportunities to interact, follow instructions, see text and hear good language models.

It is often the case that the best times for communication are the informal and social opportunities, such as snack time, nappy changing, playtime or outdoor play. Practitioners should be aware of the importance of communication at these times. This may mean offering training to other staff, such as lunchtime supervisors. It is also worth thinking about activities or routines that extend beyond the setting's day and how these can maximize a child's communication development; this may require interacting with the parents or other settings the child accesses.

Creating smaller and more nurturing spaces will make children feel secure and encourage them to communicate more. Practioners can try using 'pop-up tents', create 'talking booths' or 'talking zones'.

Case study: A crèche in a children's centre observed that the room was very visually busy and noisy and that the children did not have opportunities for quiet times. They purchased a pop-up tent for £10 and set it up in a corner of the room. The tent was filled with cushions and some loose pieces of fabric such as fur

Activity

Think about a place you have visited where your experience was negative. Write down all the things you did not like about your experience. Now think about a place you have visited where you had a positive experience. Relate this to your setting. Discuss what experience your children and parents may have when they first visit your setting. Make a plan of how you might improve on your practice. Ask parents or visitors about their experiences of visiting you and see if they can indicate any improvements.

Top tip

Have a 'three ring' policy. When the telephone rings try to answer it within three rings. This shows parents and people trying to communicate with you that you value their call.

Interaction activities

Peep po game (from birth)
Use a silky scarf or a piece of cloth. Make an animated face. Get the baby's interest by making sounds or talking to him/her. Cover your face with the silky scarf and say 'where's baby?'. Take the scarf away and say 'peep po' or 'there he/she is'. Babies love this game and begin to anticipate your reappearance. Make sure your voice uses lots of up and down tones.

Nappy changing time game
Use this time to talk face to face with the child. It is a good chance to introduce the rhyme 'round and round the garden'.

Round and round the garden like a teddy bear
(*circle your finger around the child's hand*)

One step
(*make fingers 'walk' up the child's arm one step*)

Two steps
(*make fingers walk up the child's arm again*)

Tickly under there
(*tickle child under chin or armpit*).

Spin the bottle game
Sit the children in a circle. Use a plastic bottle with a little sand or water in to make it weighted. Ask a child to spin the bottle. See who the neck end points to. The child who has spun the bottle has to name that child. For older children you can extend this to more complicated language like describing the child or saying one thing they like about the other child.

fabric. A small selection of books was put into the tent. Within an hour of this being set up a small group of children went into the tent and sat looking through the books together with the fur fabric pulled over their knees. One child fell asleep and had obviously been seeking a quiet space to relax.

Some practitioners find that their setting does maximize the time spent with each child but that the child is only with them for short periods. If this is the case, practitioners should advise parents and other carers of how to make other activities and daily routines more communication-orientated.

Interaction

Practitioners need to make sure that there are a lot of opportunities throughout the day for children to interact both with each other and with responsive adults. Some children can get by throughout a day with very little interaction and are easy to miss in a busy early years setting. Individual children need to be observed for how much interaction they have over a certain period of time. The checklist below will be useful for this.

Practitioners should make use of these observations to establish what stage individual children are at in terms of interacting. This will help plan which activities to set out, or where a child may need support from an adult. Children learn best from a good role-model; it is therefore essential that practitioners are confident in their own ability to interact.

The following checklist can be used for self-assessment, peer observations or for videoing practitioners (for the purpose of a self-audit). This can form the basis of continuing professional development. There are many resources available to help support practitioners when making observations: the ICAN *Learning to Talk, Talking to Learn* DVD is one example or see the National Strategies' 'Questioning everyday practice' materials (see the 'further reading' section on page 62).

Some of the key skills for interaction are good eye contact, turn taking, showing an interest in the other person, listening and responding. There are lots of games that encourage these skills.

Pass the parcel game

Simple turn-taking games encourage children to acknowledge others without the need for verbal interaction. Pass the parcel is a great game for children to take turns and learn to wait. Sit the children in a circle and play some music. While the music is playing the children pass the parcel around the circle (alternatively use a toy animal or another object). When the music stops the child holding the parcel can either tear a layer of paper off the parcel (or if using a toy animal toy make the animal sound) until the music starts again.

Vary the game with 'treasure bags' containing a range of objects/toys collected from the environment. When the music stops the child can pull one object out of the bag and see if they can name the object. Younger children will enjoy just taking turns and taking the objects; older children may want to name it, describe it or make the symbolic noise for the object.

Turn-taking games

There are many games commercially available which can be manipulated to develop turn-taking skills. This may be simple stacker cups where you share out the cups and simply take turns building a tower through to games like 'Pop Up Pirate' where you take turns to push a sword into the barrel and one of you will make the pirate 'pop up'. Other games that encourage turn taking include inset jigsaws, post boxes, shape sorters, skittles, and picture lotto.

Ball rolling game

This can be played between a practitioner and child, or a group of children sat in a circle all facing each other. Take turns to roll the ball to each other. Do not roll the ball until eye contact is made. This can be played with babies as soon as they are able to sit unaided. With older children, say a child's name and wait for eye contact before rolling the ball. For children at sentence level get them to describe something about the person they are sending the ball to, for example 'Jane has brown eyes.'

Bean bag game

Sit the children in a circle and put a hoop in the middle. The children take turns to hold the bean bag. The child with the bean bag has to wait until he/she hears their name to throw the bean bag into the hoop (call out lots of names and put the relevant child's name among them to check if he/she is listening).

Use animated voices to get the child's interest. Try varying this with a fast voice, slow voice, wrong names, and funny words to really capture the children's interest in listening to your voice. Alternatively, all the children can have a bean bag at the same time and they simply wait to hear their own name.

Catch a smile game

Sit in a circle. One person starts by making eye contact and smiling at someone in the circle. The person who receives the smile must choose a different person and pass the smile on in the same way. By the end of the game everyone should have given and received a smile. This game is great for adult teams or parent groups too.

Attention and listening skills

Learning to listen and pay attention is a key skill which underpins language development. Children need pay 'selective attention' to sounds in order to react to the right ones. Most children develop this selective attention at around eight months to one years old.

Did you know?

More than 90% of our communication is conveyed by non-verbal means.

Did you know?

Smiling releases chemicals called endorphins (natural pain killers) and serotonin. Together they make us feel good and can boost our immune system.

Unfortunately in today's society there are many barriers hindering this development. Children are growing up in homes with constant background noise from televisions, music systems, computers and electronic games. Listening development requires someone to be close to the child, make eye contact, speak directly to the child with minimum distractions and also to give the child chance to talk.

Many practitioners are reporting home environments where children rarely have a key adult to speak to and where they are exposed to high levels of background noise and visual distractions. This makes it even more important for early years practitioners to get the setting's environment right. Children with communication difficulties may have particular problems with listening and will need the environment to be responsive to these needs. All staff within a setting should reflect on their own practice and have opportunities to discuss this with other members of staff.

Listening activities

Musical statues
Ask all of the children to stand. Play an instrument, such as a a tambourine. While you are playing the instrument the children should walk around. When you stop playing the instrument the children must stand very still. Vary this game by introducing new rules such as when the sound stops the children must sit down or shake hands.

Stop and go game
Ask the children to stand. Explain to the children that when you say 'go' they should walk and when you say 'stop' they need to stand very still. You may need to put up your hand with a 'stop' gesture. Vary the game by giving instructions to run, jump, wriggle, hop, wave or other actions. This is a great game both for listening skills and also to teach verbs (action words). You can also give different children opportunities to be the leader and call out the instructions.

Match the sound game
Have a small range of musical instruments set out. Create a screen with a big book, box or large piece of card. Tell the children to sit on one side of the screen while you sit on the other side and play the sound of an instrument. Remove the screen. Ask a child to try and find the instrument that made the sound.

Alternatively, have two sets of instruments, one set for you and one set for the children. Ask the children to listen to you play one sound from behind the screen. The children should work out which instrument made the sound by playing their set of instruments. Remove the screen so that they can see if they are correct..

Vary the game by taking audio recordings from around the setting. This may be a tap running, a teacher talking, or a musical instrument. Play the sounds to the children and ask them to name the sound.

Comprehension

Any games that require children to follow instructions are good for comprehension development. Establish what level of understanding the children are at and try activities to take them to the next level. For example, if a child understands a few basic nouns it may be worth introducing some verbs. If a child understands one word in a sentence but not two, try to encourage two-word understanding through regular practice of games aimed at achieving this target.

Comprehension activities

Simon says game...
Use a variation of the game 'Simon says' to give instructions at an appropriate stage. Tell the children to stand in a circle. Use a puppet to be 'Simon' and say 'Simon says'. Give the instruction of the words you are working on, for example: for verbs you might use 'walk', 'run', 'hop', 'jump'; for nouns you might say 'Simon says find a pencil' and so on..

Shopping games
Set up a role-play shop. Create picture shopping lists for the children. The number of pictures on the lists should vary according to each child's stage of development. Ask the children to take their lists to the shop and use them to ask for

the items. The 'customers' must not show their shopping lists to the shopkeeper. The shopkeeper must listen and find the corresponding objects.

This activity works well with children who have listening or comprehension difficulties as they have a picture cue that can help them. It also gives the children feedback as to whether they are correct or not. If they are struggling they can share the picture with an adult or another child enhance their understanding.

Picture activities can really help children with comprehension difficulties. Use a photograph album to create a book of pictures or photographs of everyday objects and people for the children to label. Go through this daily, asking each child to find and label particular pictures to help with comprehension and expressive language.

There are a range of talking photograph albums available, which are useful to encourage families to record messages to go with the pictures.

Picture timetables
Develop picture timetables to orientate the children through the day. Start with a small number of pictures and build these up. For example, start with key pictures of arrival, snack, playing, lunch, and home times. Refer to these throughout the day. Try to use the same language to describe them so that the children learn some of the associated vocabulary. Photographs are often more effective than pictures or symbols.

Some children may not recognise pictures, so start with objects to represent the activity, such as a piece of fruit to identify

snack time, a toy to represent playing and so on. Make sure the parents know what pictures or prompts you are using so that they can introduce the same at home to continue the language learning beyond the setting.

Expressive language

Children can often get by in a setting without talking very much. Practitioners need to provide opportunities for children to express themselves and take the time to listen and respond to their attempts. There are some simple strategies that can be adopted to ensure children have chances to express themselves.

Make sure there is always someone available to listen to children when they arrive at the setting. Get down to the child's level when they are talking, make eye contact, smile and genuinely listen to what they have to say. For very young babies this may be as simple as being close, smiling and talking to the baby and then waiting for a response. Practitioners are often guilty of not waiting for a response and trying to fill every silence, try counting to five in your head whilst waiting for a response to see if the child just needs a little thinking time. Practitioners plan activities and make them available for children throughout the day; however it can be worth refraining from putting all of the essential equipment out so that children have to make requests. If a child is struggling without the equipment but has not asked yet, prompt them with questions like 'Is there something you need?', or 'What would you like me to get?'.

In the early years children find it very hard to express their thoughts and feelings. Practitioners should always listen and respond to their attempts, even if it is not the right time. For example, if a practitioner is talking to the children about birthdays and a child interrupts by saying 'I've got some new socks', the practitioner could say 'I can see your lovely socks. Did you get them for your birthday?' This will bring the child back to the topic while still acknowledging the child's interest.

Developing vocabulary is the key to enhancing both comprehension and expressive language skills. Children need to hear language in context and to hear words repeated several times (at least six times) for them to develop a wide vocabulary. Practitioners should use key words regularly throughout the day and repeat them in different contexts.

Expressive language activities

Barrier game

Barrier games are a great way to encourage communication and expressive language. Place a screen between two children or one child and a group. Give the children identical objects on each side of the screen. The child on one side of the screen must set out his/her objects in a certain way and then describe what they have done to the children the other side of the screen. Instructions may be as simple as 'get the cup and the ball' or as difficult as 'put the big red ball behind the tall green cup', depending on ability.

Feely bag game

Sit the children in a circle. Select objects and items that you would like children to learn names for. Show the children the objects; tell them what they are called and describe what you do with them. Let them touch the items and pass them round. Make a 'feely bag' out of an old pillow case or material stitched into a bag. Put one of the objects into the bag. Pass the bag around for the children to feel the object through the cloth. Can

Did you know?

There are at least a quarter of a million distinct words in the English language.

anyone remember what the item is called? If this is difficult let the children put their hands into the bag and feel the object directly; the tactile (touch) sense may help the children learn the language quicker. Lastly, pull the object out of the bag and see if the children can name it.

Clue box game

Make a small circle or flap in the front of a cardboard box. Choose a box that is big enough to put objects or pictures into. Slide an object or picture slowly past the opening of the box so that the children see part of the object, but not the whole thing, in one go. See if they can remember what the item is called.

Memory game

Introduce key words you have identified through objects and pictures. Put all the items onto a tray. Cover the tray with a cloth. See how many items the children can remember. Alternatively, for older children just take one item away and see if the children can guess which item is missing. Every time children have a guess this reinforces their vocabulary.

Follow the clue game

Find a range of objects and pictures. Hide them under a box or cushion (or for pictures, you could put a card flap over them). Give the children clues about the picture or object, such as 'It is a fruit. It is yellow. You peel it. Monkeys like to eat them.' Reveal the picture or object when the children have guessed so that they can see if they are correct. For older children, see if they can give you and the other children the clues.

Developing vocabulary through story themes

The key to this activity is preparation. Choose a story and go through the book identifying the key words. Make sure there are a range of nouns (naming words), verbs (doing words) and adjectives (describing words). Choose words that are relevant to the children's abilities. You can use some of the previous games to introduce the words before you read the story.

Read the story to the children and then re-read it asking the children to listen for a particular key word. You may want to have an object 'cue' to remind the children of the word they are listening out for. For example, if you use The Little Red Hen story, the key words may be 'hen', 'mouse', 'cat', 'corn', 'bread', and 'red'. You might choose a puppet hen, mouse, and cat and have a real corn on the cob, a slice of bread and some red fabric.

You could use these objects for the games described above before reading the story to the children. Share out the objects and get each child to listen out for their object name as you read the story. Make sure you really emphasize the word when reading the story. Read the story slowly and with lots of expression. If the child does not notice their word within the text say 'Oh listen, I have heard a key word' and repeat the word again. Make sure the objects and the book are available for the children to play with freely after the storytelling session. This allows the children to practise the vocabulary in their play and in a relaxed environment.

Developing vocabulary through role play

As with storytelling, role play is a great way to introduce new words and topics. Once you have identified your theme for a role-play area (based on observations of the children's interests or experiences) set out the area with a range of key items. Show

the children any new items you introduce and play some of the vocabulary games to introduce the new words. Tell stories that link to the role-play theme so that children hear language associated with the objects you are introducing. Carry out activities that link with the role-play theme. Make trips or provide real-life experiences that link with your role-play theme. For example, if you introduce the role-play area as a shop you may change the items for sale depending on which new words you want the children to learn. You might help them create their own shopping lists using pictures drawn or stuck on from catalogues and magazines.

You will find that when left alone to play in the role-play area the children will begin to use the words and phrases you have modelled and thus embed the language. Follow this up by asking parents to make a simple shopping list with their child next time they are going shopping together and ask them to encourage their child to ask for or find the items on the list. As a setting you may wish to follow up the activity by taking the children to a local shop to buy items for the role-play shop. The children will recognise the items they have bought and will be able to associate them with where they came from.

Sound discrimination

Good speech and reading skills develop well when children are able to discriminate between different sounds. Try the activities below to enhance children's sound discrimination skills.

Sound discrimination activities

Minimal pairs game
This game helps to fine tune listening and sound awareness. Set out a group of pictures that vary by one sound, such as 'bee', 'pea', 'sea', 'key'. Have an identical set for you to use as the answer cards. Call out one of the words and ask a child to find the correct picture. Show him/her the answer card for feedback. Make sure the children are familiar with the vocabulary before you play this game. You may need to emphasize the first sound.

You can make the level harder by listening out for word endings, such as 'bone', 'boat', 'bow', 'bowl'. You can make the game harder by covering your mouth or speaking quietly to really stretch the children's listening skills.

Nursery rhymes
Sing nursery rhymes regularly and repeatedly. It is better to introduce only a few rhymes at a time to start with. Make sure you sing the rhymes fairly slowly to start with so that the children can define the words and pick up the rhythm. Many of the commercially available tapes and CDs are sung at a rapid rate and make language learning difficult, especially for children with a delay or disorder.

Introduce a 'rhyme of the week' and give copies of the words to parents to take home. Many parents do not remember

nursery rhymes from when they were younger. It would help to record some of the songs onto a CD so that parents can also hear the tune. Explain to parents that rhymes do not always make sense but that children benefit from the rhythm and repetition and the predictability of the rhymes. Also explain that rhymes encourage children to fine tune their listening skills.

Make picture cues to represent the rhymes so that you can give children a choice. For example, have a picture of a star for 'Twinkle Twinkle Little Star' and a picture of a spider for 'Incey Wincey Spider'. Show the children both pictures and ask 'Do you want Incey Wincey (hold up spider picture) or Twinkle Twinkle (hold up star picture)?'. Encourage the children to point or name the picture they are choosing. This can be introduced with very young children from about the age of one year. As the children get older you can introduce more choices or get them to guess the rhyme by showing all or part of the picture.

Speech

All children go through a normal pattern of immature speech. Practitioners should be familiar with the ages at which children are expected to develop certain sounds (see Chapter 4). There are key signs that can help to identify those children who may be at risk of not developing certain sounds. Listen for unusual sounds; slushy or very nasal sounds are not part of normal development and may need referral to a local speech and language therapy service. Children with severe speech difficulties often have an inconsistent pattern of speech, which develops slowly. Again, it is essential to make contact with other key practitioners like health visitors and parents to discuss any concerns.

Dummies used over a long period of time can affect children's speech and language development. They can make speech sound 'slushy' and can make the child be quite 'dribbly'. Aim to reduce the amount of dummy use and try to be rid of them completely by the age of 12 months. Extended use of bottles can have the same affect.

Speech activities

Speech development is dependent on a range of skills. It involves the co-ordination of movements of the lips, tongue, teeth and palate, while maintaining breath control. There are many fun everyday games which can improve these skills and which can be built into everyday practice.

Bubbles game (for mouth movement)
This game will encourage lip rounding and control of the air stream. Get some traditional blowing bubbles or a bowl of water with washing-up liquid in it; bath bubbles are all equally useful and great fun.

Create a bubble and try different sounds and see what happens to the bubble,

E.g. 'ppp', 'bbb', 'sss', 'hhh', 'fffffffffff'. The children can experiment to see which sounds make the bubbles move the most, or even pop.

Plastic-based bubbles available from many toy stores are great for children to learn controlling their air stream. The bubbles last longer and are more robust, therefore children can blow them in different directions. Give the children directions of which way to blow the bubbles, or just let them have fun controlling the bubbles by themselves.

Straws game (for mouth movement)
Use straws to direct the air stream. You can use them to blow fluff, paper, liquids, ping pong balls, cotton wool and so on. Sit the children in a circle. Use one of the materials described above and get the children to blow it across the circle to each other. This is great fun but also a good way for children to direct their air stream ready for talking.

Mirror blowing game (for mouth movement)
Use a mirror and see if a child can steam it up with his/her breath. This teaches control of the air stream for speech.

Copy Toby Tongue (tongue game)
Use a puppet with a moveable tongue, otherwise get the children to look at your tongue and copy. The more practise children have at this game the better. Most pre-school children have little or no tongue awareness and have limited control over its movements. This story gives them a chance to practise tongue movements in a fun and safe way without even realizing they are working on their speech development.

Toby Tongue story: Tell the story and demonstrate how to move your tongue at each part of the story. It may help to use a

mirror to show children what their tongues are doing (although some children are distracted by this).

Toby tongue lives in your mouth. Your teeth are his windows and your lips are his doors. Say hello to Toby!
(*Put tongue out.*)

Can you make him clean the windows?
(*Tongue up to teeth and wipe around teeth.*)

Can you make him clean the doors?
(*Tongue around lips.*)

Toby tongue comes out of his house into the garden.
(*Put tongue out.*)

He looks up at the sky to see if it is raining.
(*Tongue out of mouth and up towards sky.*)

He looks down at the ground to see if there are any puddles.
(*Tongue out of mouth and pointing down towards ground.*)

He looks up and down the garden to try to find his dog.
(*Tongue side-to-side slowly.*)

He finds his dog who is wagging his tail.
(*Tongue side-to-side faster.*)

He decides to take the dog for a walk but the dog pulls him one way (*tongue across to one side*), then the other way. (*Tongue across the other side.*)

He falls over.
(*Push tongue straight out.*)

And lands on his head!
(*Tongue tip down at bottom of mouth inside teeth.*)

He jumps up and shakes himself down.
(*Wiggle tongue around.*)

Next, he starts to laugh then sing.
(*Say or sing 'la,la,la'.*)

And finally he closes the door and goes to bed.
(*Close your mouth.*)

See if the children can tell Toby what to do. Encourage them to explore different tongue movements and to look at each others' tongues to tune into the oral skills involved.

Making faces game
Play copy cats by taking turns to pull a funny face. The other children must try to copy the face. Encourage children to use their eyebrows, cheeks, lips, tongue to really explore mouth and facial movements. Look in the mirror at your funny face before you show the group.

Playing with sounds game
Make a set of cards with sounds written on one side and a symbol to represent the sound on the other. Laminate the cards. You may use symbols that correspond to other sound schemes you have used to avoid confusion; or you could photograph an adult making the sounds and stick these pictures to the backs of the cards to show what the lips and mouth look like while the sound is being made.

Put the cards into a bag. Ask the children to take turns picking a card out of the bag. Model the sound and then encourage the children to make the sound. You could use a puppet to vary the game, modelling the sound through the puppet.

Try the following sounds:

Encourage lips together: – 'p'/ 'b'/ 'm'
Tongue-tip sounds: 't'/ 'd'
Hissing sounds: 's'/ 'z'/ 'sh'

Top tip

Do not worry if the children cannot make all of the sounds. Make yourself aware of the developmental stages of speech (see Chapter 4) to help you identify any areas of concern.

Open-wide sounds: 'k'/ 'g'
Tricky sounds: 'j'/ 'ch'/ 'l'/ 'r'

Sound monsters game

Make a monster post box by drawing an outline of a monster and sticking it onto a shoe box. (Alternatively make the box into a post box or a different animal to encourage children to take part.)

Cut out a hole for the monster's mouth. Tell the children that the monster can only eat a certain sound. Say 'Today's sound is' and choose a sound. Have a range of sounds written onto cards. Try to have a variety, such as 'p', 'b', 't', 'd', 'f', 's', 'sh'.

Take turns to choose a card. Say the sound and ask the children to copy you. Ask the children 'Is that the monster's sound?' If it is, the children should try to say the sound and then post the sound into the monster's mouth.

Wake the puppet game

Use a puppet that the children are familiar with. Tell the children that the puppet has fallen asleep. Tell them that today he will only wake up if he hears a certain sound, such as 'sssss'.

Go around the group and ask individual children to say a sound to see if they can wake the puppet up. Every time they say the target sound the puppet will jump up and wiggle about then go back to sleep again. When everyone has had a turn you can tell them that the puppet is now 'a good listener' and that he is awake.

This is a really quick and fun game, which gets the children listening and trialling a range of sounds. This can be very successful from the age of about two years onwards and is a great game for children who are struggling with particular sounds to give them extra practice at articulating the sounds.

Sounds carry meaning game

Make a treasure bag. This can be a sparkly handbag or any interesting bag. Put in objects and toys to represent sounds, such as:

Lion: 'raaaar'
Mouse: 'ee' 'ee'
Picture of a sore thumb: 'ow'
Cat: 'miaow'
Monkey: 'oo' 'oo'
Parrot: 'oy'
Ghost picture: 'boo'

Ask the children to take turns pulling objects out of the bag. Tell them what sound the object makes, or ask the children to tell you what sound they think it makes. Allow the children to hold on to the objects. When all of the objects are out of the bag ask. 'Who has got 'raaar'?' and so on to encourage children to listen and match the sounds to the object and to try sound-making themselves.

Checklists

The following three pages contain photocopiable checklists designed to enable you to assess how communication friendly your setting is. The checklists cover:

- observing children's interaction

- observing practitioner interaction

- whether listening is a priority for the setting

Interaction observation checklist

Name of child	
Date of observation	
Time (observation began)	
Time (observation ended)	
Questions	Comments
Where was the child?	
What activity was the child engaged in?	
How many children were nearby?	
How many children did the child interact with?	
How did they interact? Non-verbal Verbal	
How did the other children respond?	

Practitioner 'effective-interaction' checklist

Practitioner behaviour	Never demonstrated	Occasionally demonstrated	Often demonstrated	Always demonstrated
Practitioner is in a good position for the child to see him/her (close and on the same level, face to face).				
Practitioner makes eye contact with the child.				
Practitioner allows the child to take the lead in play.				
Practitioner gives the child chance to start the interaction.				
Practitioner shows an interest in the child's communication through looking/copying/answering/repeating and adding.				
Practitioner gives the child enough time to respond.				
Practitioner uses language appropriate to the child's level.				
Practitioner asks questions when relevant but does not bombard the child with them.				
Practitioner makes questions open-ended to encourage the child to respond.				
Practitioner uses an animated face with an interesting voice.				
Practitioner demonstrated that communication is fun.				
Practitioner uses words familiar to the child, but introduces new words where appropriate.				
Practitioner praises the child's communication through showing an interest, smiling and acknowledging the child's attempts.				

Listening development checklist

	Always	Sometimes	Rarely
Do you minimize background noise and have quiet times throughout the day?			
Does the setting have allocated quiet areas for children to concentrate on listening?			
Are there a range of sounds for children to explore and experience on a regular basis?			
Do children get regular opportunities to talk to a key adult who is close by?			
Do all adults in your setting make eye contact with the children when they are communicating with them?			
Do you get close to children when communicating with them?			
Do you get down to the child's level?			
Do you make eye contact with children when they are talking to you?			
Do you give children time to respond?			
Do you respond to children's communication attempts appropriately?			
Do you use an interesting voice with the children?			
Do you model that you are interested in what the child is trying to say and react appropriately?			

Ages and stages

later on. Many parents were also uncertain of when to expect first words, which is generally around 12 to 14 months. Few parents knew that having regular increased noise could delay children's listening skills. Many of these myths also exist within practitioner groups and many practitioners reported having a lack of confidence in child development.

Before birth

Before birth, a baby develops rapidly from a few single cells to a fully formed baby in around 40 weeks.

The ear is formed by around 24 weeks and from this point the unborn baby may start to respond to sounds. Some scans have shown babies moving in rhythm to music and responding to the mother touching the 'bump' by as early as 27 weeks. By 32 weeks the senses are fully formed and by 36 weeks the baby recognises voices, tones and rhythms. This is often evident in new-born babies who demonstrate recognition of television theme tunes! Not so long ago, people believed that babies were born as a blank canvas waiting to be taught everything. Now we know that new-born babies have a wide range of skills at birth. Babies are born wanting to be sociable.

From birth

At birth babies can imitate simple tongue movements, recognise familiar voices and sounds and also quickly recognise the smell of their mother. The first two years of life feature the most rapid

This chapter covers the importance of knowing developmental stages in order to observe, assess and help children progress. It contains developmental charts with hints of what to look for and how to set up the setting environment to help with observations. It links to 'The Early Years Foundation Stage' and will give some hints to 'Every Child a Talker' (ECAT) practitioners of how to make observations for their child profiles.

Knowledge of child development is absolutely crucial for any practitioner working in the early years. It is the foundation of all observations, assessments and planning. Early years practitioners need to understand the typical patterns children go through in order to identify when a child is developing atypically, is advanced in their skills or is struggling with specific aspects of development. All children are different and may progress at different rates but there are key milestones that all children go through.

A survey by the programme Stoke Speaks Out in 2009, revealed that there are still many myths regarding child development. It discovered that many parents believed that picking up babies too often may spoil them. This could not be further from the truth. A young baby can never receive too much love, affection and attention. Children who have close regular contact with a main carer tend to become more confident and independent development of the brain with billions of brain cells connecting per second.

This reinforces the fact that anyone working with children in the early years has a most crucial role. The early experiences children have lay the foundations for their learning.
From birth to 12 months old, children develop at a rapid rate while physically learning to control and move all their limbs. Their communication also develops quickly from a limited range of cries and movements to understanding single words, beginning to say words and an awareness of body language and facial expressions.

During the first four months children's reflexes are evident. Reflexes are designed to protect young children but also serve to 'train' brain development. Early reflexes include watching moving objects and a preference for face shapes. These help children make social connections with their carers, which helps guarantee their survival.

What to look for
Try to notice subtle movements the baby makes, which accompany crying or signs of discomfort. This may be turning the head away to indicate 'no more' or rubbing eyes indicating signs of tiredness. Notice the pitch and volume of the baby's cries. Pain cries will be sudden, intense and loud. They may be accompanied by movements, such as drawing up the knees or stiffening of the arms. Notice if the child is startled by sudden loud noises.

When to be concerned
- If there is a lack of response to sudden loud noises.

- If the child has little or no crying to indicate needs.

- If the child shows little or no interest in people or faces.

Top tip

Children develop at different rates but generally follow a set pattern. Developmental charts can help you establish what stage children are currently at and targets they should be working towards. They are also helpful in establishing whether a child appears delayed against a 'norm' but you must observe a child over time to see how they progress.

Did you know?

Babies with hearing impairments also cry and vocalize but do not usually show startle reflexes in response to sudden noises.

Where to go for help
All children have access to a Health Visitor from birth. Children must also be registered with a General Practitioner. These professionals often have a good understanding of the family and the child's overall development and are a first point of call for any concerns. Children's centre staff may also have a good overview of the child and family development, and any services that have supported them. Practitioners should always seek permission from the parents to liaise and share information about their child. Another useful source of information is the parent-held record book, which is issued to all children soon after birth. This often contains information about the child's development history from birth and may contain information about specialist services the child has accessed.

4 to 11 months

During this phase children become increasingly mobile and more in control with their movements. They begin to learn how to manipulate their environment, particularly learning how to get attention from their key carer and the types of response to expect.

What to look for
Babies in this phase begin to develop a routine and become more effective in their range of sounds to indicate needs. A responsive carer will be tuning into the baby's needs by this phase, often from trial and error and observing the baby's behaviour. See page 45 for an overview of the stages of landguage development for this age group.

When to be concerned
- If the child's development appears to be static or regressing.

- The child shows little interest in people.

- If the child is not making any babble sounds and is showing no interest in voices or environmental sounds.

All of these signs should be followed up with detailed observations and shared with parents and a health visitor.

The following development charts can be used as a guide. If a child deviates greatly from the outline in the charts it is worth considering if all areas of development are delayed or if there is a specific area the child appears delayed in. Any concerns should be discussed with the parents, key carer or health visitor. It is vital for early years practitioners to offer experiences to enhance any areas that the child is struggling with. Remember: every child is an individual and will progress at their own rate.

12 months to 2 years

During this period children become much more competent movers and begin to manipulate their environment through communication. They have learnt to override many of their reflexes and therefore have more motor control. They begin to understand vocabulary and will be starting to use it in everyday situations. By the end of this period children should be stringing some words together in simple phrases. The way in which the key carer responds to these early communication attempts will affect the speed of communication development. See page 46 for an overview of the stages of landguage development for this age group.

30 months to 5 years

During this phase children extend the early vocabulary they have previously developed and start to use it to comment, request and converse with their peers and wider group of carers. Children learn to enjoy using language to manipulate their environment. They start to recognise that communication not only gets their needs met but that it can be used to express different feelings. How quickly this develops depends on the responsiveness of the environment and the people in it and also the opportunities to explore language through interaction and play. See page 47 for an overview of the stages of landguage development for this age group.

Case study: Ryan had been cared for daily by a child-minder since he was six months old. The child-minder had a sound knowledge of child development. At the age of 25 months Ryan was following all aspects of 'normal' development but only said a couple of recognizable words. The child-minder knew from observations that Ryan understood language well and was confident that he had good listening skills and was playing appropriately. She continued to stimulate him through a range of activities and continued to observe his progress. By 27 months Ryan suddenly began to name lots of words and within weeks of this was stringing three words together in sentences. Ryan is a good example of where development can suddenly take off in a matter of weeks.

Top tip

When observing children, ensure that you observe them in a range of different situations. Some children can learn a skill in one scenario but cannot always transfer this to other situations.

Did you know?

In normal development children understand words before they can say them.

Did you know?

The average English-speaking 17-year-old knows more than 60,000 words.

Stages of child development: Birth to 11 months

	Birth-1	0-4 months	6 months	6-11 months
General	Spends long periods asleep at this stage. Reflexes are evident, e.g. if cheek is stroked baby will turn head towards the side that is stroked.	Reflexes still evident. Recognises familiar faces, e.g. carer, when being fed.	Sits with support and kicks strongly. Bears weight on feet and bounces up and down when supported.	Pulls self to sitting position. Sits unsupported on the floor.
Understanding	Shows preference for social stimuli. Stops crying when picked up and spoken to.	Shows preference for face shapes.	Watches people's faces when they are talking. Responds to different tones of voice. Responds with arm movements to words such as 'bye bye'. Appears to recognise names and family members.	Responds when name is called.
Expressions	Can imitate basic facial gestures, such as sticking out tongue. Establishes interaction with carers through eye contact. Cries to indicate needs.	Demonstrates different cries for different needs. Smiles from about four weeks. Coos in response to smile or voice. Smiles randomly at first and then smiles become more intentional.	Babbles for attention. Sound play with familiar adults. Laughs and squeals. Babble will have a wide range of sounds, some of which are not in the child's environment.	Babbles in strings, which are beginning to sound like words.
Size of vocabulary	Zero.	Zero.	Zero.	Some early words may be forming.
Speech sounds	Makes guttural noises when content.	Gurgles and coos with a range of sounds.	Vocalizes tunefully using sing song vowels and consonant combinations. Gurgles and coos.	Babble will contain the sounds the child hears in the environment.
Looking and listening	Startled reaction to sudden loud sounds. Momentary stilling to continuous sounds.	Briefly looks at people. Shows an interest in faces. Quiets in response to sounds.	Fleeting attention to new actions, objects and events. Turns to parent's voice across the room.	Visually attentive.
Play	Passive acceptance of bath and dressing routines. Will grasp object when placed in hand.	Will grasp object when placed in hand. Long periods of staring at large shapes.	Plays speech gesture games like 'peek a boo'. Delighted response to rough and tumble play. Mouthing, inspecting, hitting and shaking objects.	

Stages of child development: 12 months to 2 years

	12 months	18 months	24 months
General	Uses a pincer grasp. Points with index finger. Can drink from a cup. Can stand without support.	Can walk alone. Can push and pull objects. Can kneel upright and walk up and down stairs with help.	Can run safely. Is able to stop and start with ease. Can throw a small ball overhand and forwards without falling over. Should be able to build a tower of about seven cubes.
Understanding	Can recognise their name and may turn when called. Should understand simple commands such as 'no' and 'bye bye'.	Should be able to recognise a range of single words in context , e.g. 'Where's the dog?' May be able to point to some body parts on request.	Should understand many more words and may understand two words together for example 'put the cup on the table'.
Expressions	Will be babbling with strings of sounds that sound like words, some will be used as real words. (These will generally be things from their immediate environment that they are familiar with.)	Babble develops into more meaningful words. These words will be used consistently but are not always clear. They will generally be words that are regularly heard in the environment and that are responded to by the main carer. Vocabulary increases depending on child's experiences and reactions from key adult.	Learns to associate words together. Can link two words together into short phrases. (To help with this children need to include a wider range of words into their vocabulary, such as action and describing words.)
Size of vocabulary	May have around five words used with some consistency. Vocabulary is related to the immediate environment.	Vocabulary grows rapidly depending on child's experiences and response from key carers. Average child will have around 10 to 20 name words (mainly nouns).	Vocabulary develops rapidly and now includes verbs (doing words) and adjectives (describing words). May have around 50 words in vocabulary. (Some children leap from a handful of words at 24 months to hundreds of words by 30 months.)
Speech sounds	Uses a simplified sound system and may often be unclear. Can use easier and more 'visual' sounds, such as 'p', 'm', 'b' ,'w', 'd'.	Speech attempts are still unclear. Makes lots of attempts to copy new words. Predominantly uses the 'easier' sounds.	May be extending use of sounds to include 't', 'k', 'g', 'n', and will enjoy playing with sounds. Still sounds unclear, especially to unfamiliar adults.
Looking and listening	Concentrates on the most powerful stimulus whether seen or heard. Will be easily distracted.	Can concentrate on own choice of activity for short periods but will be easily distracted. Adults can get child's attention for short periods of time.	Shows increasing interest in the surrounding environment and will explore. Can focus on one activity for a short time.
Play	Enjoys interaction games such as 'round and round the garden' and shows anticipation by moving excitedly.	May start to develop some imitation of simple everyday activities, e.g. pretending to drink a cup of tea. (This is often related to self rather than another person or object.)	May develop some simple role play by relating one object to another, e.g. feeding teddy as well as self.

Stages of child development: 30 months to 5 years

	30-36 months	36-47 months	48-59 months	5 years
General	Becomes more confident with movements. Should be able to climb nursery apparatus and kick a ball gently.	Will start being confident in using equipment, such as a tricycle. Should be able to build a tower of nine or ten cubes.	Will be fairly competent at walking up and down stairs. May even hop on one foot. Can copy circles and crosses and run on tip toe.	Motor skills are much more co-ordinated. May be able to co-ordinate two movements, such as standing on one foot with eyes closed.
Understanding	Can generally identify objects by their use, e.g. 'Which one do you drink from?' Enjoys familiar stories and nursery rhymes. Most understanding is related to the here and now.	Develops from understanding two key words to three key words within a sentence. May understand past tense. May start to comprehend more complex language, such as prepositions and describing words.	Becomes more confident understanding three to four words in a sentence, e.g. 'Put the cup behind the chair.' Recognises that past is different from present; time concepts develop.	Develops an awareness of grammatical aspects of language. Generally understands everyday conversations. Can appreciate jokes, riddles.
Expressions	Vocabulary extends into simple phrases of about three to four words together. (These will be 'telegrammatic', i.e. key words without all of the joining words.)	Sentence length extends to about four to six words together. Demonstrates an awareness of grammatical rules but over uses them, e.g. 'I goed to the park.'	Sentences continue to grow in length to about five to eight words together. Constantly asks questions. Can give an account of recent experiences and events (but may still be grammatically immature).	Utilizes language learned to relate simple stories using past, present and future tense. Sentence length will increase to around eight words per sentence. Enjoys playing with words learned.
Size of vocabulary	Rapidly increases to around 200 words, some of which extend beyond the here and now.	Vocabulary continues to increase rapidly to around 500 words or more.	Should know more than 1000 words.	May know between 1500-2000 words. (This is still reliant on the experiences the child has been exposed to.)
Speech sounds	Speech may still be unclear. Words will have sounds at beginning, middle and end but not always the correct sound. Can generally indicate the correct number of syllables.	More difficult sounds may be emerging such as 's', 'f', 'z', 'v'. Speech may still be unclear but there will be a consistent pattern.	Sounds 's', 'f', 'z', 'v' will be used more consistently and regularly. Clusters of sounds may still be difficult to say, e.g. 'sp', 'st', 'pl', 'br'.	Uses most sounds correctly. May still make mistakes with 'th' and 'r' and more difficult clusters of sounds or longer more complicated words, e.g. 'squirrel'.
Looking and listening	Concentration improves and increases. Can attend to an adults choice of activity. Curiosity increases but there is still little awareness of danger.	Enjoys listening to stories and will listen eagerly. Enjoys repetition of the same stories. Can often recognise if you alter the text of a story.	Can listen to longer stories. Can shift from 'listening' to 'doing' within an activity.	Looking and listening is usually well established.

Communication observation

Use this photocopiable sheet to observe individual children's speech and language development.

Name of child	
Date of observation	
Which activities does the child choose?	
Are these mostly verbal or non-verbal activities?	
Are there any particular people the child chooses to interact with?	
Describe how the child interacts in relation to: ▪ eye contact ▪ facial expressions ▪ vocalizing ▪ gesturing ▪ touching ▪ pointing ▪ taking turns ▪ talking	
How effective are the child's attempts to communicate? How do others respond?	
When does the child seem most interactive?	
Is communication in line with rest of the child's development?	

Observing children through play

Use this photocopiable sheet to record background information on individual children to supplement your observations.

Name of child	
Date of birth	
Date of observation	
Age on observation	
Does the child have siblings? If so, how many? Are they older or younger?	
Which language(s) is/are the child exposed to?	
Describe the child's home experiences of play.	
How much experience has the child of playing with other children?	
Are there any cultural practices that the child and their family follow? Such as taboo objects/religious beliefs which may affect play?	
Are there any medical conditions that need to be considered? Such as hearing loss, physical difficulties.	
Other comments:	

Involving parents and carers

This section covers why parents are important in their children's learning and provides ideas to get parents involved. The chapter includes photocopiable handouts and games for parents to try. For the purpose of this section, the definition of 'parent' will mean any person offering the key caring role for the child and may include foster carers, adoptive parents or any other adults with parental responsibility.

Many studies have indicated that the influence of parents is paramount to a child's development. The Effective Provision for Pre-School Education (EPPE) study (2004) stated that it 'is not who parents are but what they do that makes the difference' in their child's development. Parents often feel unsure of how to fulfil their role. The majority of parents love their children and want to do their best for them but lack the knowledge and skills of how to develop children to their full potential.

The EPPE study highlighted a range of key ways in which parents could help their child's development. These included:

▪ Reading to and with children

▪ Singing songs and rhymes

▪ Going on visits

▪ Painting and drawing

▪ Creating opportunities to play with friends

▪ Going to the library

▪ Playing with letters and numbers

The extent to which practitioners work with and involve parents will depend on the setting's relationship with parents. Remember that parents also need support to prepare for separating from their child; involving them in their child's learning can help to ease this anxiety. Make sure the parents

know the setting's key routines including who their child will be handed over to, where they need to go and what they are expected to do. Many parents feel anxious about arriving at a new setting and about leaving their child. If they have had negative experiences themselves this will also raise their anxiety.

Preparing parents for the setting

Offer parents and carers informal opportunities to look around the setting, this may include coffee mornings, chances to see children performing, family-learning workshops, creative sessions and fundraising events. It is helpful for parents to meet practitioners in an informal role for them to feel confident to share any concerns and to build up a relationship.

If possible, conduct a home visit (prior to a child attending the setting) to meet the parents or carers on their terms. Home visits reveal much more information about a child's background in five minutes than in a whole academic term in a setting. During a home visit a practioner can see the opportunities a child has had prior to attending the setting; it can also help parents and carers feel more able to share information. Offer written information about what is expected of them, where they need to go, names of staff and so on (but be mindful of the parents and carers who cannot read English or have poor literacy levels). Make sure there is someone who can talk through this information if necessary. Some settings create a DVD of what the setting looks like and demonstrate a typical day in the setting. This is a great way to prepare both parents and children, and is a resource they can revisit again to develop discussion about the setting.

Some settings have purchased a plasma screen for their entrance hall to play footage of the children undertaking activities within the setting, showing parents and carers what the children have been doing. A photo album highlighting key staff, information about the activities and routines of the day are great ways to share information with parents.

Involving parents

Create an area for parents so that they know where to go for information about the setting and other relevant useful information such as 'giving up the dummy'. This may be an accessible wall, noticeboard or even a room. Think about what this space tells parents about how they are valued.

Find out what information parents would find useful and monitor how effective the use of the information is. Judge this by putting ten leaflets in each plastic wallet and noting each week how many remain. Try personalising information boards, give each child their own post box for parents to check daily to see if they have any post. Ask parents to supply any relevant news that they would like to see on the notice-board, this may be celebrating the birth of a new child or community events that they wish to share.

Settings often report difficulty in getting parents to come in and be more involved. Many parents work full time and tight schedules mean that they do not have enough time to stay and chat about their children. In these instances, practitioners should review the types of communication strategies provided by the setting. These may range from leaflets; informal chats; telephone contact; home-setting diaries; performances; open days/evenings; parent evenings; fund-raising events; coffee

Ideas for parents to use at home

Pyjama treasure hunt game

This is a good game to help your child learn to listen and also helps encourage him/her to get ready for bed. Near to bedtime hide your child's pyjamas somewhere in the house. Give your child clues of where to look. For example 'You need to go in the bathroom' or 'Look behind the basket'. Keep your language at your child's level and make the clues harder or easier accordingly. Praise your child when they find the pyjamas and reward them by lots of hugs and a bedtime story.

Treasure chest game

Go on a treasure hunt around the house with your child. Encourage your child to find five items; for younger children this may be things that interest them and for older children use a theme, such as five red items. Put the items into an old shoe box. Seal up the box and say it is the treasure. The following day, see how many items your child can remember before you open the box together. Talk about the items as you pull them out. If five items is easy, try adding more or add more unusual objects to help your children learn new words.

Shopping game

Before you go out shopping together, help your child make a simple shopping list. This might be pictures of items you want them to get or labels taken off the real items for your child to match. When shopping, ask your child to find the items that are on the shopping list. Encourage them to tick all of the items on the list as they are collected. Let your child put the items on the conveyor belt and pass the money to the shop assistant. This game will keep your child occupied and helps to teach children about interacting with others.

What can you hear? game

Spend one minute every day with your child, stopping all activity and listening. Tell each other what you can hear. It may be the washing machine, dogs barking or cars passing. This is a great way to assess your child's listening skills.

Easy I spy game

When you are walking or driving along see if your child can guess what you are looking at. Give simple clues such as 'I can see something that barks.' When your child gets the hang of the game, see if he/she can give you clues.

Stories and props

Choose one of your child's favourite stories. Go around the house and garden and collect things that link to the story. For example, in relation to Cinderella you may wish to collect a high-heeled shoe as the glass slipper, a toy mouse, and some sparkly fabric to represent the dress. Use these to talk about the words in the story. Next time you read the story use the objects as props to help you tell the story. For example hold up the sparkly fabric when you talk about Cinderella's dress. Encourage your child to help you find the objects and to explore them in the story. It doesn't matter if you go off at a few tangents as long as your child is hearing the language and is learning new words.

---

mornings/evenings; workshops; trips; and formal family-learning sessions. Offering a wide range of communication methods will ensure that all parents and carers are involved in some way. These communication methods should also be used to promote the setting's key messages. Consider what language the parents speak and read, their literacy levels, their availability (especially if they work) and any other commitments they have, which may reduce their contact with the setting.

Parents are more likely to engage if they have a key person they can relate to. They form a connection or attachment with a named person and then feel confident enough to talk to them and share information. If the key contact person cannot be consistent make sure parents know who is available and when. Introduce a communication book for staff to write down any concerns or questions asked by parents and share these with appropriate colleagues so that they are dealt with quickly and efficiently. Simple measures like having labelled photographs in the entrance hall can make parents feel more relaxed and confident.

There will always be some parents who choose not to engage; this cannot be forced. As with any relationship, there needs to be trust, opportunities and reasons to communicate with each other. These parents will engage more with time, once they feel they are ready, or when they feel the need.

Practitioners can also try using these useful communication methods:

- Make a keyring with memos on. This might be a list of names, contact numbers or things to bring in on a certain day. Use coloured cards to write or print the messages on. Cut them out and laminate them. Punch a hole in each card, then link them together with a keyring loop. This is a practical way for parents to keep important information about the setting close to them.

- Make a door hanger template with a list of 'don't forget' messages. This may be left blank for parents to write their own messages on, or you may supply one with key messages already written on it. Messages might include 'read me a bed time story' or 'ask me about my day' and for older children may include items that they need to bring in.

- Many parents use mobile phones and these might be a more effective way of getting parents involved. Try text messaging parents information, such as invitations to events or reminders about news items. Text messages can also be used to reassure parents that their child has settled or is feeling fine if they have returned after an illness.

It is worth asking parents about what links they would like to make with practitioners and the setting and the types of communication formats they would find most useful. Asking parents for this information will make them feel valued and listened to; therefore improving their relationship with the setting.

The questionnaire on page 56 can be photocopied and used as a starting point, but please note that this does not replace the need to develop a face-to-face relationship with parents.

Key messages for parents

There are a range of key messages that parents need for them to support their child's communication development. Practitoners can take one key message at a time and promote them through handouts, workshops or newsletters. They can also form part of the child's induction to the setting.

- **The role of the parents:** The first message is that parents are the most important people in their child's development. Many parents believe that children will start to learn when they get to school or nursery and are happy to wait until that time. Parents need to know that what they do and how they communicate with their child will have the most effect on how their child develops. Talk to parents about how they can encourage quiet times, listening times and how they can encourage talking in all everyday activities, even the household chores.

- **Create opportunities for talking:** The second message is to create opportunities for talking throughout the day. This might be giving the child choices of what to wear or eat for breakfast, counting the stairs, naming the shopping, or naming the clothes on the washing line. Parents need to know that learning to talk and communicate is one of the most important skills children learn and they do this by following the model of the people around them.

- **Make time for communicating and talking:** Lifestyles nowadays are so busy and hectic that it becomes easy to overlook the importance of sitting down together, face to face, and simply talking. This can be done at mealtimes around the table and at other times throughout the day. Parents worry that they will 'spoil' their children by giving them their attention. In fact the opposite is true. Children who have regular opportunities to be close to their parents and be listened to develop more quickly and therefore become more independent.

- **Limit dummy/bottle use:** Most parents do not know that using a dummy or bottle excessively can delay their child's speech development and may make speech 'slushy' or more 'dribbly'. Many parents think that if they do not give their baby a dummy, he/she will go on to suck their thumb. There is no evidence to support this view. Some children will thumb suck whether they have ever been given a dummy or not. It is worth sharing information with parents about the link between glue ear and dummies/bottles. This way they can make an informed choice over dummy and bottle use.

- **The importance of a listening environment:** Encourage parents to create a listening environment at home. This can be achieved by having times of day when the television, computer games and music are not on. The whole family need to sign up to this. Once the environment is quiet parents will be amazed at how much better the child will concentrate for playing and talking. Encourage parents to be good 'listening models' and assess their priorities. For example, if the mobile phone rings at the same time as the baby cries, which will they respond to first? Parents need to remember that a phone call can wait but a child cannot; every experience shapes the child's developing brain and these experiences will last for their whole life.

■ Use the visit to show the parents that you are approachable and friendly so that they will be more confident approaching you in the future.

If possible, it is better for two practitioners to attend a home visit together so that one can concentrate on the child whilst the other concentrates on the adults.

Conducting a home visit

Many practitioners now conduct home visits as part of a child's induction to the setting; play and learning teams from children's centres may also provide this type of service. Home visits may take some practitioners out of their comfort zone. Here are some basic tips to help make home visits run smoothly.

■ Preparation is essential. Find out which other agencies already support the family. Identify any risks associated with a home visit. These may range from an unfriendly dog to an aggressive male partner in the home. If you are unsure, obtain consent from the parents to liaise with their health visitor or children's centre to investigate any concerns. Find out what languages the family speak and if necessary take an interpreter along with you.

■ Use the visit to give and gain information. Observe what types of play opportunities the child has, who the significant people are in the child's family are, how the parents interact with the child and whether there is increased background noise or evidence of dummy and bottle use.

■ Ask parents about how the child developed from birth; who the child interacts with; what languages the child is exposed to; what toys the child prefers to play with; and whether the child has been to other settings or sees any other practitioners.

■ Ask about the child's general health and any reasons why the child might have difficulty attending your setting.

■ Give the parents information about the routines within your setting, names and contact details of key people, and key activities. Encourage them to ask questions and always leave some written information that summarizes what you have said. For parents who cannot read English you may find using a DVD of your setting more effective as you can watch this together and go through the key things.

■ Find out if the child has any appointments or other agencies involved. Note their names and contact details and ask the parents for consent to liaise with them.

■ Share information about parent opportunities within your setting. Ask how they would like to communicate with you (use the parent questionnaire on page 56).

Working effectively with parents

Communication opportunities offered to parents	Potential or existing barriers	How might barriers be overcome?

Questionnaire for parents

We would like to share information with you about your child's learning and progress. Your opinions are valuable to us. Please fill in this questionnaire to help us improve our service to you.

1. How would you like us to share information with you? (Tick all that apply.)

   ☐ Regular conversation

   ☐ Newsletter

   ☐ Letters

   ☐ Internet/e-mail

   ☐ Home-setting diary

   ☐ Parents' evening

   ☐ Open evening

   ☐ Telephone

   ☐ Text messages

   ☐ Other – please state _____

2. What kind of information would you find most useful for us to share? (Tick all that apply.)

   ☐ What activities your child has been doing

   ☐ How well your child is progressing

   ☐ What friends your child has made

   ☐ What activities your child likes best

   ☐ What activities your child does not like

   ☐ Any concerns we have

   ☐ Ideas to support your child's learning at home

   ☐ Other – please state _____

3. How well do you feel we communicate with you?

   ☐ Excellent

   ☐ Good

   ☐ Could do better

   ☐ Poor

4. Please give us any ideas to improve our contact with you:

Many thanks for completing this questionnaire.

Top tips for talking

- Make time for talking and listening to each other.

- Take time to listen to your child. Ask questions but don't bombard your child with them and give them time to answer.

- Keep your language at your child's level.

- Ask open-ended questions so that you extend language, e.g. ask 'What did you have for dinner?' rather than 'Did you have beans for dinner?'

- Look at your child when he/she is attempting to communicate with you.

- Keep background noise to a minimum to help your child develop listening skills (have TV times but not all the time!)

- Include brothers and sisters in conversations and encourage them to interact with their younger siblings, but don't let them take over!

- Get down to your child's level when you are communicating. If your child is sitting down crouch down to be at the same level.

- Make eye contact with your child when they are talking to you.

- Value every attempt your child makes at talking, even if the attempts are unclear.

- When your child speaks in early simple sentences, repeat the sentence back but add a word, e.g. if your child says 'Daddy car' acknowledge this with 'Yes it's daddy's red car'.

- Show your child that you value their attempts to talk by giving them your full attention. It helps to turn off your mobile phone or television for part of the day so that you are not interrupted.

- Everything you do is a language learning opportunity. Talk to your child while you are doing your everyday chores so that they learn the language you use at home.

- If you have any concerns about your child's communication development discuss this with your child's Health Visitor/ school nurse or staff at the nursery or setting.

Communication development in a multicultural society

This section provides hints and tips for working with children who speak a language that you may not be familiar with. It covers how communication may develop in different languages and how to conduct relevant observations. It emphasizes the importance of reading children's non-verbal cues to get an understanding of their communication levels and suggests some tips of how you might start to introduce English to these children.

We are living in a constantly changing environment that has many rich and varied cultures. Britain has seen huge changes in the past ten years. Some parts of Britain, which have previously had predominantly white British populations, are now made up of a variety of families from different cultural and language backgrounds.

When working with bilingual children practitioners need to have a toolkit of strategies that can be adapted to suit the child's needs. Being bilingual should be seen as a gift, not as a handicap. Bilingualism is the norm for the majority of the world. The term 'bilingualism' means that the child has access to more than one language. Many children from different language backgrounds miss out on referral to specialist services because their difficulties remain undetected by practitioners who do not have the skills to assess these children properly.

There are a number of points and tips that can help practitoners working with bilingual children. Remember much of this good practice is relevant to any cultural background, including children who are from an English-speaking background.

Preparation for working with bilingual children

When working with bilingual children practioners need to find out what life is like for them beyond the setting. (This also applies to all children). It is important to know who their main attachment figures are and how well they have prepared the child for attending the setting.

Top tip

If a child is developing well with a home language other than English, it should be relatively easy to teach English to the child later on. This is because the child learns the building blocks for language and has the desire to communicate. Ensure that parents realize the importance of speaking their home language to the child.

Did you know?

Approximately two thirds of the world's population are bilingual.

Children need to feel emotionally secure and confident before they can move on with their language and learning skills. If a child is from a different cultural background, find out who cares for them, how many carers there are, who will be collecting and dropping off the child and any family circumstances which may affect the child's emotional state. Identify what languages the child has been exposed to and at what stage of language development the child is at. Some children are 'simultaneously' bilingual, meaning that they learn two languages at the same time. Some have 'sequential' bilingualism, where they learn one language first and then other languages are introduced later. Some children are mistakenly labelled as bilingual but do not have access to more than one language, and some are delayed in their home language but this is often undetected.

It is essential to find out which language the child is exposed to and by whom. For example, the mother speaks one language to the child and siblings speak another. It is important to ask the parents if they have any concerns about any aspect of their child's development as they are more familiar with how the home language should develop. These concerns need to be judged against routine observations as many parents do not have a good overview of how 'normal' development takes place.

Practitioners need to be confident and familiar with normal patterns of child development. Motor, fine motor development, perceptual skills and hearing behaviours have little variation across the world. Although languages differ in grammar and vocabulary there are still some basic similarities between them. All languages begin with interaction skills, such as seeking out eye contact, body language and facial expressions. It is important to find out if there are any particular cultural practices for non-verbal behaviour, such as avoidance of eye contact in

school-aged children as a sign of respect. The easiest way to observe a child's communication development is through their non-verbal behaviour.

Tips for assessing bilingual children

- Watch how the child makes contact with other children. Will he/she tolerate other children close by? Does the child make any attempt to include others and if so is this verbal or non-verbal? This will tell you a lot about the child's social development.

- Observations should also include watching how quickly the child picks up routines. Watch to see if the child follows others and if he/she is recognizing the simple routines of the day. Some settings have triggers to indicate a particular time of day, e.g. a bell to indicate 'tidy-up time'. Watch over a period of time to see how quickly the child recognises the trigger and responds to it. This can give you a good insight into their comprehension skills.

- If you have a bilingual support assistant get them to ask the child to do some simple tasks to see how well the child is comprehending language. Notice if the assistant needs to give additional clues such as gesture, repetition or eye pointing. This may indicate that the child is struggling to understand the words spoken to him or her.

- Observe the child's attempts to talk. Which language(s) does the child choose? Are the attempts clear? How well do the other children respond? Are the attempts sounds, single words or sentences?

Helping bilingual children to settle in

Home visits are very valuable. They give practitioners an insight into a child's world. Home visits should be used to investigate what play opportunities a child has, what the home routine is and any barriers to development, such as increased background noise, busy environments or lack of time with a responsive carer.

When conducting home visits, practitioners should phrase questions to parents in non-threatening and open-ended ways. For example, to find out about play experiences ask the parent what toys and games the child likes best and what things he/ she likes to do at weekends; this is more likely to get an accurate and honest response than than asking if the child plays and if the parents have any concerns. Be aware that some homes are deceptive. It may appear that there are no toys available in the home but it may be that the parents have taken the practitioner into the 'best' room reserved for visitors, and that the toys are hidden in a different room or in a storage box under the sofa.

Tips for home visits

- Take along pictures or photographs to help get over any language barriers. These can include photographs of what the setting looks like, routines of the day, and of staff to help demonstrate the environment to the family. They will also give you a chance to introduce new vocabulary to both parents and children.

- Some settings produce a DVD of their setting to prepare the child for things they will see and experience. If this can be left in the home it is a great opportunity for children to revisit and discuss with parents things that have gone on throughout the day.

- If you know what language the parents speak and have an interpreter available, take them along. This will be beneficial because the parents will feel more confident in the transition from home to setting and will be able to ask questions. You will also be able to find out detailed information about the child's development history.

It can help children to settle in if they hear some of their home language spoken in the setting environment. If possible, try to learn a simple phrase such as 'hello' in the child's language. If there are interpreters or bilingual workers available, ask them to spend some time with the child in simple everyday conversation to make the child feel more secure.

Try to obtain some books, posters and games in other languages. Make sure role-play areas contain some objects familiar to the child's home background.

Language development in bilingual children

Some people assume that a child will learn to speak late if he/she is exposed to more than one language. There is no research evidence to say that bilingual children speak later. Some parents also worry that speaking a home language will hold their children back. This is not true. Home languages are part of our cultural and social history. It is important that a child is able to communicate with the people who are most significant to the child; in the first instance this is the parents and carers, family and friends.

Many families are embarrassed by the fact that they cannot speak English. Families need to feel proud of their cultural heritage and realize the richness their experiences can bring to the child and the setting. Show families how much their culture is valued by acknowledging diversity, taking an interest and passing on the key message that their culture is important to the setting. If the parents are really keen to learn English, direct them to a local 'English as a second language' course, which are often run at children's centres and local colleges.

Be aware that some children learning English for the first time may go through a normal silent phase. This can often

Did you know?

A child's brain is rapidly forming from birth and slows down by puberty. It is therefore much easier to learn a second language during childhood. For speech sounds to be most accurate it is best if a child acquires the second language before adolescence.

Top tips for parents

- Aim to be consistent with the language you speak to your child.

- Try not to mix languages within a conversation.

- Provide lots of opportunities for your child to learn language.

- Read or tell stories to your child in your home language, this will help your child learn new vocabulary and language structures.

- Create opportunities for your child to use all the languages they hear.

- Use the language you are most competent in with your child.

- Try to take your child to places where they will have some exposure to English before they start nursery or school, e.g. the local shops or post office (this will help your child get used to hearing English spoken in context).

last up to six months and is perfectly normal. During this phase children are absorbing the new language, noticing the similarities and differences and developing their confidence non-verbally at first. Use observations to help assess whether a child is going through this 'normal' silent phase or if he/she is delayed in expressive language skills. It is also normal for some children to become non-fluent in their home language as they learn to use a second language, such as English. This should normally pass as the child becomes more proficient in the second language.

Language difficulties

There are various reasons why a child from a non-English background may appear to experience language difficulties. These can include:

- limited experience of English

- hearing difficulties

- limited experience of play

- developmental delay

- medical problems

- learning difficulties

- environmental factors, e.g. bereavement, separation, home stresses

- lack of a good communication model at home

- lack of opportunity to practise communication in a range of contexts

- silent phase whilst the new language is being absorbed.

If a child is not following a normal pattern for any area of development, or if the parents express concern, this will require further investigation. If the child shows continued signs of distress for long periods of time or does not pick up the routine of the setting this may also need to be looked into. In these instances, it is worth discussing concerns with the a health visitor and the parents/carers. If a child is not developing their home language in a normal pattern, this may require referral to a Speech and Language Therapist, but note that referrals are not appropriate for children who have established a first language and are just slow to develop English as a second language. These children can usually progress through good early years practice and lots of language-rich experiences.

When teaching English as a second language to a child, the practitioner should introduce lots of gesture and non-verbal communication, alongside talk, to support the child's learning process. Various games, routines and picture timetables can help the child pick up English vocabulary. Ensure that the child has time to listen and respond and try to involve the parents as much as possible.

If a child is not developing well in the home language, look at whether the child is delayed in any other areas. If so, carry out a series of observations and discuss any concerns with the child's parents and health visitor; they may need a referral to a paediatrician.

If it is just the child's speech and language that is delayed, ask the parents if they understand the child and if the child understands them. Carry out observations to look at how well the child interacts non-verbally. If he/she is using lots of gestures

Did you know?

Some languages do not have words to express particular concepts that occur in the English language. For example, a parent may have only learned colour names at school and only knows the names for these in English. They will therefore put the English words into a sentence using their home language and this will appear as both languages mixed together. This is fairly common and is something to be aware of when working with children from other language backgrounds.

and facial expressions and is sociable this is less of a concern than a child who is withdrawn and is struggling to interact. Ensure that the child has a lot of opportunities for quiet times and introduce stories and games at a stage-related level rather than an age-related level.

Speech development

When a baby is born, he/she is capable of producing any human sound from any language. By the age of six months, a baby's babble takes on characteristics of the language the child hears in the immediate environment. The majority of brain growth and development occurs within the first three years and it is in these early years that the foundations of language learning are at their best.

Regarding speech development, a child learning a second language, such as English, in the pre-school years is far more likely to speak that language with accurate sounds. If the child learns the second language after puberty it is likely that he/she will represent the second-language sounds with their first-language sound system; as a result they may struggle to pronounce certain words or have a strong accent.

While it is vital that a child is taught the dominant home language first (so that his/her social needs are met), it is also helpful to expose the child to English speech so that correct pronounciation is developed.

Children who have not been exposed to hearing English early on may find it hard to represent sounds through writing, for example some languages have no 'clusters' of consonants such as 'sp' or 'pl'. Despite this, we teach children phonics and expect them to blend sounds very early on in our education system and this may cause problems for children who have no internal representation of these sounds in their home language. It is important to have some background knowledge of a child's first language to help plan and support the child's English learning, alongside all other aspects of development.

Much of the information in this section is similar to the advice in all the other sections. This is because communication basics and good practice cut across all cultures. If practitioners follow best practice for communication development, they will be able to support all children that they work with.

Further reading

Government publications

Bercow (2008) *Review of Services for Children and Young People (0-19) with Speech, Language and Communication Needs.* www.dcsf.gov.uk/bercowreview

The Early Years Foundation Stage (2007). www.teachernet.gov.uk/publications

Rose, J (2009) *Independent Review of the Primary Curriculum: Final Report.* DCSF

Books

Baker C (2000) *A Parents' and Teachers' Guide to Bilingualism.* 2nd edn. Clevedon, England

Bergman R (2008) *Stories for Talking.* QEd Publications

Bruce T (2005) *Early Childhood Education.* Hodder and Stoughton

Bruner J (1983) *Child's Talk: Learning to Use Language.* WW Norton, New York

Buckley B (2003) *Children's Communication Skills*

Chilvers D (2006) *Young Children Talking: The Art of Conversation and Why Children Need to Chatter.* Early Education

Delamain C, Spring J (2000) *Developing Baseline Communication Skills.* Speechmark

Hart B, Risley T (1995) *Meaningful Differences in Everyday Parenting and Intellectual Development in Young American Children.* Brookes Publishing

Hart B, Risley T (1999) *The Social World of Children Learning to Talk.* Brookes Publishing

Johnson M (2007) *Helping Children Hang onto Your Every Word.* QEd Publications

Lees J, Urwin S (1997) *Children with Language Disorders.* 2nd edn. Wiley Blackwell

Lindon J, Kelman K, Sharp A (2008) *Play and Learning in the Early Years.* Step Forward Publishing

Locke A, Beech M (1991) *Teaching Talking.*

Locke A (2006) *One Step at a Time.* Network Continuum Education

Lynch C, Kidd J (2003) *Early Communication Skills.* Speechmark Publishing

Macintyre C (2007) *Understanding Children's Development in the Early Years.* Routledge

Palmer S (2006) *Toxic Childhood.* Orion.

Pound L (2008) *How Children Learn.* Step Forward Publishing

Sheridan M (2008) *From Birth to Five Years: Children's Developmental Progress.* Routledge

Sonnet H, Child P (2002) *Stepping Stones to Success.* Positive press

Sunderland M (2006) *The Science of Parenting.* DK Publishing

Sutherland H, Hall A-M (2003) *Deaf Friendly Nurseries and Pre-Schools.* NDCS

Sylva K, Sammons P, Siraj-Blatchford I, Taggart B (2003) *The Effective Provision of Pre-School Education Project.* Institute of Education, London

Whalley M (1997) *Working with Parents.* Hodder and Stoughton

Williams D (1995) *Early Listening Skills.* Speechmark Publishing

Journals

Beals D (1997) Sources of support for learning words in conversation: evidence from mealtimes. *Child Language* 24: 673-94

Biemiller A (2003) Vocabulary needed if more children are to read well. *Reading Psychology* 24: 323-35

Bishop DVM, Adams (1990) A prospective study of the relationship between specific language impairment, phonological disorders and reading retardation. *Journal of Child Psychology and Psychiatry* 31

ICAN Talk series (2007) The cost to the nation of children's poor communication. Issue 2 (info@ican.org.uk)

Lindsay G, Dockrell J, Mackie C, Letchford B (2002) Educational provision for children with specific speech and language difficulties in England and Wales. Cedar Institute of Education, University of London

Locke A, Ginsburg J (2003) Spoken language in the early years: The cognitive and linguistic development of three to five-year-old children from socio-economically deprived backgrounds. *Educational and Child Psychology* 20

Organisations and Websites

Association for all Speech Impaired Children: www.afasic.org.uk

British Stammering Association: www.stammering.org

Cleft Lip and Palate Association: www.clapa.com

Communication Trust: www.thecommunicationtrust.org.uk

ICAN: www.ican.org.uk

London SIG Bilingualism: www.londonsigbilingualism.co.uk

Mother Tongue Matters: www.mothertonguematters.com

National Deaf Children's Society: www.ndcs.org.uk

Siren Films: www.sirenfilms.co.uk

Stoke Speaks Out: www.stokespeaksout.org

Talk To Your Baby: www.talktoyourbaby.org

DVDs

Annette Karmiloff- Smith Beckman *Baby it's You: The First Three Years*.

Hello Dad: Infant Communication for Fathers
shop@dad.info. Tel 08452242009

ICAN (2007) *Learning to Talk, Talking to Learn*

Siren Films *Attachment in Practice*

Siren Films *Firm Foundations in Early Literacy*

Siren Films *Learning Through Play: The Three to Four Year Old*

Siren Films *Life at Two*

Siren Films The Wonder Years: *First Year Development and Shaping the Brain*

Acknowledgments

I have had a very privileged career working with a wide range of innovative and enthusiastic professionals.

Special thanks are due to the Stoke Speaks Out team who are a constant source of knowledge, expertise and support.

Also thanks to the Speech and Language Therapy department from North Staffordshire Community Healthcare, especially Karin Evans, for nurturing my career and giving me so many opportunities to develop.

I have received valuable experience by working alongside my colleagues in Early Years for Stoke on Trent City Council, particularly Michelle and Rob Johnstone.

My personal thanks also go to Cris, Joe and Jessica for their endless support and encouragement in all that I do.